EXCEPTIONAL STORIES

from the Lives of Our Apostles

EXCEPTIONAL STORIES

from the Lives of Our Apostles

Compiled by Leon R. Hartshorn

Published by
Deseret Book Company
Salt Lake City, Utah
1973

Library of Congress
Catalog Card No. 72-90346

ISBN Number 087747-486-9

Copyright 1972
by
Deseret Book Company
Second Printing 1973

LITHOGRAPHED BY

DESERET NEWS PRESS

N THE UNITED STATES OF AMERICA

Table of Contents

Elder Rudger Clawson

Elder Matthew Cowley

President Jedediah M. Grant

Elder Alonzo A. Hinckley

President Anthony W. Ivins

President Brigham Young, Jr.

Biographical Sketch

ELDER MELVIN J. BALLARD

Elder Ballard was born February 9, 1873, at Logan, Utah. His father was Henry Ballard; his mother was Margaret McNeil.

Elder Ballard's father served as the bishop of the Logan Second Ward for more than thirty-nine years.

In 1896 the Church conducted an experiment in missionary work.

Elder B. H. Roberts was called to tour and speak in some of the leading cities of the United States. George D. Pyper, who had a fine tenor voice; Melvin J. Ballard, who had a beautiful baritone voice, and Edward P. Midgley, organist, were called to accompany him.

Elder Ballard was called as mission president of the Northwestern States Mission with headquarters in Portland, Oregon. He assumed his new position on May 1, 1909.

He served as mission president for ten years until his call to be an apostle on January 7, 1919. He was ordained by President Heber J. Grant. He was forty-five years old at the time of his call.

In 1925 Elder Ballard was called on a mission to South America.

Elder Melvin Joseph Ballard died on July 30, 1939.

Elder Ballard's son, Melvin R. Ballard, has paid the following appropriate tribute to his father:

Melvin J. Ballard was a man of prophetic vision and deep spirituality, which was controlled by a well-balanced mind; thus imparting confidence in what he said. There was something majestic and satisfying in his conception of the Gospel and the place which man had in the eternal Universe. All his admonitions and exhortations were permeated with hope and good cheer. His words banished doubt and inspired faith and stirred men to righteous action. This combination of talents made him one of the most popular and powerful exponents of the restored Gospel in this latter day dispensation. (Melvin R. Ballard, *Melvin J. Ballard—Crusader for Righteousness* [Salt Lake City: Bookcraft, 1966].)

MELVIN J. BALLARD

"Give Me Children, Else I Die"

Melvin Joseph Ballard was a child of promise. He was carried beneath his mother's breast during a period of poverty, of depression, of crop failure, and of sorrow. She had given birth to six children. Two were taken in death while in the first year of their lives, just ten days apart. They were twins, a boy and a girl. Sorrow and sickness had weakened her physical strength, and in the years to follow she lost several children who were born prematurely. Her heart was sore; her arms were empty; and again the life of her unborn child was threatened. Many days and weeks she was bedfast, but like Rachel of old her heart yearned for a child, and she cried unto the Lord, "Give me children, else I die."

Her husband had taken the children a block away to see a parade, and while he was gone she raised her trembling body from the bed and crawled and locked the door so that she might pour out her soul to God on her knees in prayer. She called to remembrance her willingness to bear children. . . . She supplicated the Lord for help. She felt that she had done all that was in her power, and she asked to know her standing in His sight.

God hearkened unto her prayer, and a comfort was given to her. She saw no person, but a voice spoke plainly to her saying, "Be of good cheer. Your life is acceptable, and you will bear a son who will become an apostle of the Lord Jesus Christ."

In due time her child was born. She did bear a son, her last son, and he was named Melvin Joseph. His life was precious in the sight of his father and mother, and they recognized in him a choice spirit. He was also honored by his brothers and sisters, although they did not know of the promise given about him.

Ballard, *Melvin J. Ballard—Crusader for Righteousness* (Bookcraft), pp. 26-27.

MELVIN J. BALLARD

"Take This to Your Father"

The 18th [May, 1884] found a line of members outside Bishop Henry Ballard's home as he wrote recommends for his ward members. The day was warm and pleasant, and Ellen, Henry's nine-year-old daughter, was chatting with friends on the sidewalk outside the house when two elderly men approached, walking in the middle of the street. One of the men called, "Come here, little girl." As Ellen hesitated, the stranger pointed to her and said, "I mean you." Placing a newspaper in her hand, he said: "Take this to your father. Give it to no one else. Go quickly and don't lose it."

Henry's wife, Margaret, now picks up the story. "Ellen came in and asked for her father. I told her that her father was busy [writing recommends] and asked her to give me the newspaper she had in her hand so that I might give it to him. She said, 'No, the man who gave the paper to me told me to give it to no one but Father.' I let the child take the paper to her father."

Henry quickly took in the situation. The newspaper was the *Newbury Weekly News* containing "Wanderer's" jottings from Thatcham churchyard—names and other genealogical details for sixty or so now-dead acquaintances of Henry and his father. Who had brought it? Rapidly quizzing Ellen he hurried outside, went around the block searching and questioning. In that sparsely settled community, where all the inhabitants were known to each other, no neighbors had seen the two strangers. They were never found. This disappearance of the messengers was itself cause enough to wonder, but perhaps even more impressive was the date on the newspaper—May 15, 1884. In an era long before the advent of air transportation and when mail took several weeks to get from England to western America, this newspaper had made the journey in three days!

The next day Bishop Ballard took the newspaper and recited the facts to President Merrill, president of the Logan Temple, who concluded: "Brother Ballard, someone on the other side is anxious for their work to be done and they knew that you would do it if this paper got into your hands. It is for you to do the work, for you received the paper through messengers of the Lord." To their great joy, the Ballards received baptism and endowments in the temple for all the people he had listed. "Wanderer" never knew in this life the great work his vacation ramblings had made possible.

Ballard, *Melvin J. Ballard—Crusader for Righteousness* (Bookcraft), pp. 16-17.

"Tied to His Mother's Apron Strings"

The crowd he [Melvin J. Ballard] went with enjoyed outings and canyon trips, dancing and picnics. Melvin enjoyed very much of this fun and was not curtailed in his wholesome amusements. But when these parties were planned on Sundays, or weekends which included Sundays, his mother was grieved, but never forbade his participation. She would say, "Melvin, you do as you please. You know as well as I do what is right and what is wrong; but if you go, you will displease both me and the Lord." Serious reflection was always given to his mother's counsel. Because he refused invitations, he was ridiculed many times; and it was said of him, "He is tied to his mother's apron strings." Later in life he said, "Thank God my mother's apron string was strong enough to hold me."

Ballard, *Melvin J. Ballard—Crusader for Righteousness* (Bookcraft), pp. 30-31.

"What Does Stephen Think About It Now?"

I remember going from Nauvoo over to the capitol of the state, Springfield, Illinois, and holding a conference of missionaries from northern and southern Illinois. And I remember that two of us, myself and companion, who had charge of these two districts, applied to the governor of the state. It was considerable nerve, I will grant you; but in my youth I was zealous and was willing to ask for anything—and we had the nerve to ask the governor of the state of Illinois to give us the State Capitol building in which to hold a "Mormon" conference. Well, he happily surprised us by granting us the privilege, and that without a dollar's cost to us. We were permitted to use the Hall of Representatives; and before large numbers of people, who filled that hall, we discoursed upon the principles of the glorious, restored gospel and bore witness and testimony that Joseph Smith was a prophet of God, and that the Book of Mormon was true. My soul was thrilled, because, I remember, as I looked about that place and saw on the one side of the rostrum a life-sized portrait, full length, of Abraham Lincoln and on the other side a life-sized portrait of Stephen A. Douglas, I could not help but wonder in my soul, What does Stephen think about it now? For it was in this identical place that Stephen A. Douglas delivered his address on the "Mormon" question, while running for the presidency of the nation, and proposed that if elected he would apply the knife to this pestiferous cancer "Mormonism," which was a growth upon the body politic, and he would burn it out and destroy it. Well, he did not live long enough to do that, and "Mormonism" came back to his home, into the very place where he was eulogized by his associates for his stand against this work, and yet, here we were, peacefully, at the kindness of the officials of that state, permitted to declare again the glad news that the God of heaven had spoken to Joseph Smith, and that we had a message for all men.

Conference Report, 1921, p. 100.

"His Arms Laden With Books"

The older Indians told us, on several occasions, the story of their first meeting with Elder Ballard. They said that one day Elder Ballard was traveling east across Montana by train. As the train approached a very small town which was just being settled, Elder Ballard noticed, from the train window, a huge encampment of several hundred Indians. Their teepees were pitched in a large circle on the prairie. Elder Ballard was instantly interested and felt a keen urge to visit with them. He obtained stopover privileges and left the train to spend the day at the encampment, with the intention of proceeding on his journey the next day. He hired a horse and buggy, secured an interpreter, and drove out to the Indian encampment at a place called "Chicken Hill," on the banks of the Missouri River.

Elder Ballard left the horse and buggy and with the interpreter walked out among the people. As he approached them, they showed signs of great emotion and began talking excitedly to him. They seemed to be asking him for something. The interpreter explained that many of the Indians had seen, in dreams, a white man come among them. Always he had his arms laden with books which were of great value to the Indians from their contents. As soon as they saw Elder Ballard, they recognized him as the man they had seen in their dreams and they wanted the books he was supposed to bring to them.

Of course, Elder Ballard was exceedingly impressed and told them briefly the story of the Book of Mormon and of its significance to them. He told them he must go on his way now, but that he would return soon to bring them the books and teach them more.

When Elder Ballard returned to the town he felt impressed to buy two lots in the newly laid-out town, which he obtained for a very low price. When he returned a short time later the lots had skyrocketed in price to such a figure that he was able to sell them at a tremendous profit. The money thus obtained was used to buy building materials and some acreage further out of the town, in fact, at "Chicken Hill." There a boarding school and a chapel were built, and the Lamanites were given their Book of Mormon and were taught the Gospel, as well as general school work. Many of the Indians joined the Church there, and today their descendants and many others are firm in the faith. Great spiritual manifestations occurred in this particular place, as the writings of Elder Ballard relate. Many were the healings, and many the spiritual gifts that were made manifest among the Indians. . . .

One such instance was told to us by an Indian called "Looking." He was a young boy when Brother Ballard came among his people, and he had been blind since birth. When he heard that there was a "Mormon Prayer Man" (as the Indians called the missionaries) on the reservation, he begged to be taken to Elder Ballard that he might be blessed to receive his sight. Elder Ballard administered to him, and through the power of the priesthood and the child's simple, sincere faith, his sight was restored and he was appropriately given the name of "Looking." In gratitude, Looking insisted on giving the hay from his small field each year to help feed the Church livestock at Chicken Hill.

Ballard, *Melvin J. Ballard—Crusader for Righteousness* (Bookcraft), pp. 55-57.

"The Biggest Crop of Wheat"

At a stake quarterly conference of the Taylor Stake, which was held in Raymond, Alberta, Canada, Elder Melvin J. Ballard was the visiting authority. He had spoken inspiringly, during the various sessions of the conference, but there seemed to be an unexpressed desire pervading the conference for a blessing from the lips of this great man. Elder Ballard remarked about this and felt impelled to say what is here recorded. "I advise you brethren to plant every available acre of wheat land that you have, even if you have to stubble it in, and I promise you that the rains will come and that you will harvest the biggest crop of wheat ever known in the history of this country." This prophecy was made in the month of May, at a time when the Canadian farmers feel that they have gone beyond the date when crops can be planted which would mature before the early frosts come, but the brethren took Elder Ballard at his word. So strong was the spirit, that they were moved upon to plant every available acre they owned. Elder Ballard had said that the rains would come, but it went for some time, and the rains did not come, and it seemed that the grain would rot before germination.

The brethren began to despair and some felt to complain that Elder Ballard had made a mistake this time, that he had spoken out of emotion of his heart and had not been prompted of the Lord. But the rains did come in greater abundance than anyone had probably witnessed in that locality for many years. The fields were in the southern parts of the province of Alberta, Canada.

The grain germinated and grew to a height of more than six feet in some of the fields. Early frosts came and went throughout the western provinces in Canada, and when the Canadian Pacific Railway published its crop report in December of that same year, it showed that where the Latter-day Saints were living, the early frost had not affected their wheat, and they were about to garner the greatest wheat crop in the history of that country up to that time. Many fields of wheat harvested eighty bushels to the acre, and truly it was a bounteous return, a literal fulfillment of the prophecy made by Elder Melvin J. Ballard.

Ballard, *Melvin J. Ballard—Crusader for Righteousness* (Bookcraft), p. 90.

MELVIN J. BALLARD

"He Took Me Into His Arms and Kissed Me"

I bear witness to you that I know that the Lord lives. I know that he has made this sacrifice and this atonement. He has given me a foretaste of these things.

I recall an experience which I had two years ago, bearing witness to my soul of the reality of his death, of his crucifixion, and his resurrection, that I shall never forget. I bear it to you tonight, to you, young boys and girls; not with a spirit to glory over it, but with a grateful heart and with thanksgiving in my soul. I know that he lives, and I know that through him men must find their salvation, and that we cannot ignore this blessed offering, that he has given us as the means of our spiritual growth to prepare us to come to him and be justified.

Away on the Fort Peck Reservation where I was doing missionary work with some of our brethren, laboring among the Indians, seeking the Lord for light to decide certain matters pertaining to our work there, and receiving a witness from him that we were doing things according to his will, I found myself one evening in the dreams of the night in that sacred building, the temple. After a season of prayer and rejoicing I was informed that I should have the privilege of entering into one of those rooms, to meet a glorious Personage, and, as I entered the door, I saw, seated on a raised platform, the most glorious Being my eyes have ever beheld or that I ever conceived existed in all the eternal worlds. As I approached to be introduced, he arose and stepped towards me with extended arms, and he smiled as he softly spoke my name. If I shall live to be a million years old, I shall never forget that smile. He took me into his arms and kissed me, pressed me to his bosom, and blessed me, until the marrow of my bones seemed to melt! When he had finished, I knelt at his feet, and, as I bathed them with my tears and kisses, I saw the prints of the nails in the feet of the Redeemer of the world. The feeling that I had in the presence of him who hath all things in his hands, to have his love, his affection, and his blessing was such that if I ever can receive that of which I had but a foretaste, I would give all that I am, all that I ever hope to be, to feel what I then felt.

Bryant S. Hinckley, *Sermons and Missionary Service of Melvin J. Ballard* (Salt Lake City: Deseret Book Co., 1949), pp. 155-56.

MELVIN J. BALLARD

"His Great Heart Almost Breaking"

It is written in the scriptures that God so loved the world that he gave his Only Begotten Son to die for the world, that whosoever believes on him, yes, and keeps his commandments, shall be saved. But this sacrament did not cost us very much—freely given are all these glorious privileges, and I am reminded of a statement by one of our great writers, running something like this: "At the devil's booth are all things sold. Each ounce of dross costs its ounce of gold." (J. R. Lowell, "Vision of Sir Launfal.")

It is heaven alone that is given away. It is only God that may be had for the asking. While we give nothing, perhaps, for this atonement and this sacrifice, nevertheless, it has cost someone something, and I love to contemplate what it cost our Father in heaven to give us the gift of his Beloved Son, that worthy Son of our Father, who so loved the world that he laid his life down to redeem the world, to save us and to feed us spiritually while we walk in this life, and prepare us to go and dwell with him in the eternal worlds.

I think as I read the story of Abraham's sacrifice of his son Isaac that our Father is trying to tell us what it cost him to give his Son as a gift to the world. You remember the story of how Abraham's son came after long years of waiting and was looked upon by his worthy sire, Abraham, as more precious than all his other possessions; yet, in the midst of his rejoicing, Abraham was told to take this only son and offer him as a sacrifice to the Lord. He responded. Can you feel what was in the heart of Abraham on that occasion? You love your son just as Abraham did; perhaps not quite so much, because of the peculiar circumstances, but what do you think was in his heart when he started away from Mother Sarah, and they bade her goodbye? What do you think was in his heart when he saw Isaac bidding farewell to his mother to take the three days' journey to the appointed place where the sacrifice was to be made? I imagine it was about all Father Abraham could do to keep from showing his great grief and sorrow at that parting, but he and his son trudged along three days toward the appointed place, Isaac carrying the fagots that were to consume the sacrifice. The two travelers who accompanied them were told to remain while Abraham and his son started up the hill.

The boy then said to his father: "Why, Father, we have the fagots; we have the fire to burn the sacrifice; but where is the sacrifice?"

It must have pierced the heart of Father Abraham to hear the trusting and confiding son say: "You have forgotten the sacrifice." Looking at the youth, his son of promise, the poor father could only say: "The Lord will provide."

They ascended the mountain, gathered the stones together, and placed the fagots upon them. Then Isaac was bound, hand and foot, kneeling upon the altar. I presume Abraham, like a true father, must have given his son his farewell kiss, his blessing, his love, and his soul must have been drawn out in that hour of agony toward his son who was to die by the hand of his own father. Every step proceeded until the cold steel was drawn, and the hand raised that was to strike the blow to let out the life's blood, when the angel of the Lord said: "It is enough."

Our Father in heaven went through all that and more, for in his case the hand was not stayed. He loved his Son, Jesus Christ, better than Abraham ever loved Isaac, for our Father had with him his Son, our Redeemer, in the eternal worlds, faithful and true for ages, standing in a place of trust and honor, and the Father loved him dearly, and yet he allowed this well-beloved Son to descend from his place of glory and honor, where millions did him homage, down to the earth, a condescension that is not within the power of man to conceive. He came to receive the insult, the abuse, and the crown of thorns. God heard the cry of his Son in that moment of great grief and agony, in the garden when, it is said, the pores of his body opened and drops of blood stood upon him, and he cried out: "Father, if thou be willing, remove this cup from me."

I ask you, what father and mother could stand by and listen to the cry of their children in distress, in this world, and not render aid and assistance? I have heard of mothers throwing themselves into raging streams when they could not swim a stroke to save their drowning children, rushing into burning buildings, to rescue those whom they loved.

We cannot stand by and listen to those cries without their touching our hearts. The Lord has not given us the power to save our own. He has given us faith, and we submit to the inevitable, but he had the power to save, and he loved his Son, and he could have saved him. He might have rescued him from the insult of the crowds. He might have rescued him when the crown of thorns was placed upon his head. He might have rescued him when the Son, hanging between the two thieves, was mocked with "Save thyself, and come down from the cross. He saved others; himself he cannot save." He listened to all this. He saw that Son condemned; he saw him drag the cross through the streets of Jerusalem and faint under its load. He saw that Son finally upon Calvary; he saw his body stretched out upon the wooden cross; he saw the cruel nails driven through hands and feet, and the blows that broke the skin, tore the flesh, and let out the life's blood of his Son. He looked upon that.

In the case of our Father, the knife was not stayed, but it fell, and the life's blood of his Beloved Son went out. His Father looked on with great grief and agony over his Beloved Son, until there seems to have come a moment when even our Savior cried out in despair: "My God, my God, why hast thou forsaken me?"

In that hour I think I can see our dear Father behind the veil looking upon these dying struggles until even he could not endure it any longer; and, like the mother who bids farewell to her dying child, has to be taken out of the room, so as not to look upon the last struggles, so he bowed his head, and hid in some part of his universe, his great heart almost breaking for the love that he had for his Son. Oh, in that moment when He might have saved his Son, I thank him and praise him that he did not fail us, for he had not only the love of his Son in mind, but he also had love for us. I rejoice that he did not interfere, and that his love for us made it possible for him to endure to look upon the sufferings of his Son and give him finally to us, our Savior and our Redeemer. Without him, without his sacrifice, we would have remained, and we would never have come glorified into his presence. And so this is what it cost, in part, for our Father in Heaven to give the gift of his Son unto men.

Hinckley, *Sermons and Missionary Services of Melvin J. Ballard*, pp. 151-55.

"He Was My Son Before He Was Yours"

Hasn't the Lord a right to call us home? Aren't we first of all His sons and daughters? I remember a father being unwilling to reconcile himself to the death of his only son. One day in the mountains he said to me that he had sought the Lord saying, "Why have you taken my boy, my son, my hope, my pride from me?" And there came to him the whisperings of the Spirit: "He was my son before he was yours. I loved him more than you will ever know how to love him, but if you are faithful I will give him back to you." And that father was reconciled. He was reconciled that God has a prior claim. When God calls us it is our business to say, "The Lord giveth and the Lord taketh away; blessed be the name of the Lord." That is all we can do, and if we will desire it we will overcome and rise triumphant and victorious over all our sorrows. If we can only submit ourselves to that providence we will have peace in our hearts.

Hinckley, *Sermons and Missionary Services of Melvin J. Ballard,* p. 274.

"Mother, Don't Forget Me"

An evidence that those in the Spirit World know of the work we do here in the Temples was related by President Wood of the Alberta Temple. While sealing a group of children to their parents, in the midst of the ceremony he felt an impression to ask the mother who was present, "Sister, does this list contain the names of all your children?" She said, "Yes." He began again but once more he stopped and asked if the list named all her children. She told him there were no more children. He attempted to proceed, but a third time was impelled to ask: "My Sister, have you not lost a child whose name is not on this list?" Then she said, "Yes, I do remember now. We did lose a little baby. It was born alive and then died soon after. I had forgotten to put its name down." The name was given, and then it, being the first born, was named first and all were sealed to the parents.

Then President Wood said: "Everytime I started to seal the children I heard a voice say: 'Mother, don't forget me,' and I could not go any farther." The appeal was made each time until the omission was discovered.

Church News, January 20, 1940, p. 2.

"A Great Sorrow"

As told by Lucile Ballard Madsen

One of the dearest memories is that of a loving father's care in time of sickness. If I awoke in the night, feverish and frightened, my father would be there instantly to soothe and comfort me. A glass of water, his hand on my brow, his calm, assuring conversation, and, above all, his faith-inspiring presence were all that were needed to pull my through any crisis.

In connection with the death of a loved one, I am reminded of a great sorrow which came early in Father's married life. My brother, Kenneth, a beautiful, dark-haired, brown-eyed boy, just younger than I, was stricken with rheumatism when above five years of age. For nearly a year he was confined to his bed. During this time it was my Father's practice in the morning before he went to work, at noon when he came for lunch, and again in the evening to hold this little boy, entertaining him for hours with song and story. Anyone who has been through a similar experience knows the great love that develops between parent and child. Kenneth seemed to improve steadily, and by early spring we were hopeful that he would be completely cured by summer. Instead, he caught measles from a visitor, and it was too much for his little heart. He died, much to our grief—especially that of my father. Several weeks after his burial I came upon Father, unseen by him, sobbing as if his heart would break. Only those who have heard a strong man cry will know how it impressed a child of seven.

Hinckley, *Sermons and Missionary Service of Melvin J. Ballard*, pp. 31-33.

Biographical Sketch

ELDER ADAM S. BENNION

Adam S. Bennion was born in Taylorsville, Utah, December 2, 1886, the son of Joseph Bushnell and Maryann Sharp Bennion. He graduated from the University of Utah in 1908 with a Bachelor of Arts degree. From 1909 to 1911 he was an English instructor at the L.D.S. High School in Salt Lake City. The following year he received his Master of Arts degree from Columbia University. From 1917 to 1919, he was an assistant professor at the University of Utah. In 1919, he became Superintendent of Church Schools and served until 1928. During this time, he was also professor of education at Brigham Young University. After studying at Chicago and the University of California he received his Doctor of Philosophy degree.

Elder Bennion was asked by the Church Historian's Office to complete a biographical blank which asked for "Missions filled, when called and where." Elder Bennion wrote, "No formal call, but active in New York in 1911-12, Chicago 1916, Berkeley 1922-23."

He married Minerva Young in the Salt Lake Temple on September 14, 1911. They are parents of five children.

He was called to the Twelve April 1953. He was ordained

an apostle April 9, 1953, by President David O. McKay. A high-light of his ministry was his tour of ten mission fields in Europe between April and September 1956. He traveled over 31,000 miles. He summed up the trip as follows: "Those five months have been the most enriching and inspiring of my life."

He died February 11, 1958, at age sixty-six.

Among other things President McKay said the following about Adam Samuel Bennion at his funeral services:

"It has been truly said that the mass of men worry them-selves into nameless graves while here and there a great unselfish soul forgets himself into eternity. Our departing brother was one of those great unselfish who forgot himself for others and won immortality."

ADAM S. BENNION

"Give Me Work"

God does not always answer prayers miraculously. He often shapes events so naturally that we may scarcely recognize His hand in our welfare. But He is our Father—He will help us in the hour of need if we only will ask of Him as of a father—honestly and sincerely. Here is an extract from the journal of Brother Horace H. Cummings, Superintendent of Schools of The Church of Jesus Christ of Latter-day Saints, which shows with perfect clearness that God will bless His servants when they trust in Him and attempt to do His will:

"When I was old enough my father put me to work in the Deseret Mills near Salt Lake City in the finishing department. He told all of his sons that they might have one tenth of their wages and all their over time to spend as they pleased, while he took the rest to help maintain the family. My wages were nine dollars a week and fifty cents a night for working over time until nine o'clock.

"I saved most of my money and when about eighteen years of age I had enough to attend school at the Deseret University. Unfortunately, I was unable to register until the beginning of the second term and by the end of the third term circumstances forced me to quit. My father and oldest brother were both called on missions and that meant for me to leave school and keep the family.

"For any other reason, it would have been a matter of the greatest regret to have to leave school after going only two terms, or half a year, but it rather appealed to me as an honor that had come to us. So I quit school and began looking for work. Being the last of February or the first of March, there was little to be found to do. I visited the stores, the shops, the trunk factory, and made inquiries to find work on some of the nearby farms.

"Night after night I would come home with no prospect of work until I began to be discouraged. The baby was sick and mother was not very well, and the stock of family provisions was getting decidedly low. I began to feel that something must be done.

"Before being called on his mission, my father had torn down the rear part of our old home which was a small adobe hut, and had begun to build a commodious home for us to live in. He was only able to finish one room of the new house, however, so we were living in parts of both houses.

"The day that the situation reached the climax, I went back into the closet of the new house and there knelt before the Lord in prayer. Now, of course, I had prayed to the Lord many times to give me work, but this time I had a peculiar, earnest determination to get what I wanted. I prayed with such earnestness that I cried. I fear my prayer was somewhat of a complaint, for I told the Lord He had called my father and brother to preach His Gospel and left me to support the family; that I had looked and looked for work and could not find any.

"To my great satisfaction, that very day saw an answer to my prayer. Two school trustees from the county were in need of a teacher in their district and had come to the city to get one. On making inquiry of Dr. John R. Park, the president of the university, where I had been attending, they had been referred to me as a suitable person to teach their school and after a short conversation they engaged me at $60 a month."

Adam S. Bennion, "What It Means to Be a Mormon," Deseret Sunday School Union, 1917, pp. 69-71.

"Two Years He Was an Honor Student"

The two following incidents, related by the principal of one of Utah's high schools, illustrate clearly the difference between a repentant and a self-justifying attitude. Two boys had been caught stealing—one had taken some money from another student's locker, and the other had stolen some tools from the manual training department. It is a regrettable fact that stealing should be found in American schools where every possible advantage is given to boys and girls, practically free of charge. But there are students who seem to have little self-respect and little respect for the rights of others.

The boys were called into the office and each one was interviewed separately. The boy who had taken the money was resentful. He said that he was not the only boy in the school who was stealing. Why did not the principal find the others and punish them too? Anyway, he felt that he had a right to take money if a fellow didn't know better than to leave it in a locker that wasn't locked.

The boy who had taken the tools felt altogether different. He was ashamed to think that he would lower himself to the level of a thief. He explained that he knew better than to steal but he had seen the tools lying around, they were just what he needed in doing some work at home, he couldn't afford to buy them, and thinking that perhaps they would never be missed, he took them. When he reached home, he could not make proper explanation to his parents and he was sent back to the school to be disciplined.

The principal was anxious to help both boys—he not only wanted them to finish their schooling—he wanted them to learn one of life's greatest lessons—that honesty is one of the grandest principles in the world. He explained to them that they would have to appear before the teachers of the school, make a statement of the whole affair, and give assurances that such actions would never be repeated.

The boy who had stolen the money flatly refused. He would rather quit school than, as he called it, "be disgraced." The law of the school was enforced and he was asked to withdraw. He left the school with defiance in his soul and with a sort of determination that he would get even with somebody—though he didn't seem to know just who it should be.

Out of the school he found that he had lost the respect of his old comrades, and the new ones who took their places were of a far inferior sort. He soon went from bad to worse until when last heard of he had been sent to the State Industrial School where he might be prevented from committing further crime.

The boy, on the other hand, who had taken the tools agreed to do as the principal required. It was a hard thing to do, of course. In fact, it was the hardest he had ever encountered. He not only was ashamed for what he had done, but how could he ever look those teachers in the face again? But feeling really sorry for the offense, he found courage to take the penalty. He was so manly and frank about it that every one of the teachers, who heard his confession, came to admire him more than ever before. They became his friends and took particular pains to help him find and develop his better self. When he was graduated from the school two years later he was an honor student— respected by every student who knew him. The humility of repentance had led him into a new life. Let us remind ourselves of that beautiful passage in the Doctrine and Covenants, Sec. 112, the tenth verse: "Be thou humble, and the Lord thy God shall lead thee by the hand, and give thee answer to thy prayers."

Bennion, "What It Means to Be a Mormon," pp. 80-83.

"A Prayer Circle Was Held"

Many people of the world today read of the miraculous healings recorded in the New Testament and remark that it must have been glorious to live at a time when the power of the Lord was so manifest in the world. They realize that the Savior had the gift of healing . . . today just as well as in the days of the Savior or of ancient Israel. Through the Holy Priesthood, wonderful things have been done since the organization of The Church of Jesus Christ of Latter-day Saints.

"Miss Charlotte E. Dancy, Superintendent of Nurses at the L.D.S. Hospital, came to Salt Lake City several years ago and became interested in the Gospel and finally was convinced of its divinity, but before baptism, was stricken down with a case of blood-poisoning.

"She had at her command the best medical and scientific skill in the state; all the splendid doctors who knew her, were ready to lend their best efforts; trained and competent nurses were present night and day, with every convenience and aid the splendidly equipped L.D.S. Hospital could furnish. Without an exception all who attended her said it was impossible for her to recover.

"For days she lay unconscious. She was loved and respected by all who knew her and was even revered by the nurses and by them was looked upon as a sweet, gentle, intelligent loving mother. They wanted her to live and a prayer circle was held, at which every nurse, who could be spared from active duty in the hospital, joined in that special service held at the Nurses' home and with the Elders implored the gracious Father to spare her life for service in the world. To see the girls dressed in white, united in faith, bowing in prayer, pleading for the life of one so dearly loved, was an impressive, beautiful sight never to be forgotten.

"Soon her temperature changed, her consciousness was restored and her recovery brought joy and gladness to all who knew her. She lives as a monument of faith in the true and living God and of His wonderful power to heal; and today she is a ray of sunshine, a teacher of rare ability, a consistent, faithful, Latter-day Saint."

Bennion, "What It Means to Be a Mormon," pp. 76-77.

ADAM S. BENNION

"Thank God for America"

Recently I attended in an adjoining state a testimonial in honor of the outstanding young man in his community. He was to be presented a medal of distinction. The man who was chosen to make the presentation asked the indulgence of the crowd while he told the story of the young man who was to be honored. This was his story:

There was a time in this town when a widow was left with a group of children and little to go on. Neighbors offered to help but she said she wanted to try to hold them together. And, like other noble ones of her sex, she did. She carried on by doing the washing for the community. And this young man, distinguished here tonight, is the "kid that gathered up the bundles for her to wash"!

As I shook his hand to congratulate him after the presentation, I asked him what he would have said could he have put into words what was in his heart.

"Only this—thank God for a mother who cared enough to hold us together.

"Thank God for America—the land in which a kid like me has a chance."

Church News, June 20, 1942, p. 8.

ADAM S. BENNION

"I Don't Believe I Said Thanks"

I do not think I remember anything more vividly than I do the story of one boy who broke down completely in his testimony. He said, "You know, I did not know what was going on at home, and when I got ready to leave, Mom said she was going to get me a fine suitcase. So we went down and looked over the luggage. I picked up the piece that I wanted, and when I picked it out she went into her pocketbook and pulled out six and a half books of S & H Green Stamps that she had been saving through the years for the day when her son would go on a mission."

And then as he broke down completely, he said, "The thing that troubles me today is that I don't believe I said thanks." But he said thanks in our meeting. That boy will never be the same again and I just hope that some of his gratitude rubs off through what I say so briefly today upon the heart of that good woman.

Conference Report, October 1956, p. 33.

"William Clayton"

When you gather in this edifice, [Tabernacle] you must think of the faith of men who from 1863 to 1867 toiled to build it—to 1870 to complete the balcony. As you look at the pipes in this great organ, you must be mindful that some of them were made possible only because the pioneers discovered certain kinds of timber three hundred miles to the south.

Do you know what William Clayton was doing when he wrote that *Come Come Ye Saints?* It was on the 15th of April between Nauvoo and Winter Quarters one of the toughest trips that any people ever took. I beg of you to remember that six hundred people lost their lives in those three hundred miles. He had been sick much of the time. Pick up his journal and read the first twenty pages—the little journal of William Clayton. He had been ill. His wife, Diantha, was still ill—too ill to travel. As you read those twenty pages, you will notice how often he was writing a letter to be sent back to his wife, hoping that she would be well. Then came the glad news that she had given birth to a son, she herself too ill to move. She struggled against the mumps. He himself was sick, but the morning, I love to read this—the morning the word came that he had a son—notice the practicality of it—he said they had been spending the day in a search for, "Henry Terry's horses are missing. They've been hunted all day, but are not found yet. This morning I composed a new song, 'All Is Well'. I feel to thank my heavenly Father for my boy and pray that he will spare and preserve his life and that of his mother, and so order that it be soon that we may be together again." He asked President Brigham Young, "Could they not send back and bring her along?"

President Young said, "You may."

I tried to conjure up last night that as William Clayton talked to Brigham Young about the new song he had just written, whether either one of them could ever had imagined, even in fancy, that a hundred years later 379 voices of the choir would take that same hymn and sing it to 60,000 people in Europe, and yet they did it. . . . That's faith in its fulfillment.

Conference Report, October 1955, p. 118-19.

Biographical Sketch

PRESIDENT GEORGE Q. CANNON

Elder Cannon was born on January 11, 1827, at Liverpool, England, the son of George Cannon and Ann Quayle.

As a boy, he immigrated from England to the United States with his parents who had been converted to the Church. His mother died at sea.

Two months after the assassination of the Prophet Joseph and Hyrum, George Q. Cannon was ordained a seventy and chosen secretary of the quorum. (His father had died shortly before.) Elder Cannon served missions to California, Hawaii, and the Eastern United States and England. He was ordained an apostle on August 26, 1860, at thirty-three years of age.

He served as President Brigham Young's private secretary.

Elder Cannon served as president of the *Deseret News*.

He was sustained as a counselor to Brigham Young on April 8, 1873. He was called to be first counselor to President John Taylor on October 10, 1880. Elder Cannon also served as first counselor to President Wilford Woodruff and President Lorenzo Snow.

He was a brilliant scholar and editor and a voluminous writer.

George Quayle Cannon died on April 12, 1901, at Monterey, California.

GEORGE Q. CANNON

"Whittling and Whistling"

In the aftermath of the prophet's martyrdom, the state of Illinois revoked the Nauvoo City Charter, thereby leaving the city unprotected by law. This condition naturally attracted unsavory strangers who hoped to capitalize on this absence of law enforcement. George Cannon tells how the boys his age carried on an effective voluntary defense against possible troublemakers to the Saints:

It was, and still is, a common practice among Yankees, when engaged in conversation or in making a bargain, to take out their pocket knives and commence whittling; frequently, also, when engaged in thought they indulge in the same practice, accompanying the whittling by whistling. No person could object, therefore, to the practices of whittling and whistling. Many of the boys of the city had each a large bowie knife made, and when a man came to town who was known to be a villain, and there for evil purposes, a few of them would get together, and go where the obnoxious person was, and having previously provided themselves with pine shingles, would commence whittling. The presence of a number of boys, each whittling with a bright, large bowie knife, was not a sight to escape the notice of a stranger, especially when these knives came uncomfortably close to his body. His first movement, of course, would be to step back and ask what this meant. The boys would make no reply, but with grave faces, keep up their whistling. What could the man do? If he was armed, he could shoot, but the resolute expression of the boys' faces, and the gleaming knives would convince him that discretion was the better part of valor. The most we ever knew them to do was to stand for a while and curse and threaten. . . . then they would walk off, followed by a troop of boys vigorously whittling and whistling.

Although in telling this story, Brother Cannon avoided stating that he was one of these boys, in the above account he slips and says "we." This pronoun and the apparent delight with which he tells the story are pretty good evidence that he was a participant and enjoyed being one.

Lawrence R. Flake, *George Q. Cannon: His Missionary Years* (Unpublished Doctoral Dissertation, Brigham Young University, August 1970), pp. 23-29.

GEORGE Q. CANNON

"When You Get As Old As I Am"

George Q., now sixteen, found employment with the *Times and Seasons* edited by John Taylor, with whom he lived. The thoughtful youth was known to some of the principal men of the city because of their having visited Liverpool and been entertained at his home there. Doubtless he came to the attention of others, also. But observant and possessed of an almost perfect memory, he soon came to know all the leaders and many of the people even if they did not know him.

While learning the typesetting and the printing trade, an incident occurred that revealed his attitudes. Some of the prominent men of the community were apostatizing from the Church, John C. Bennett being an outstanding example, because of immorality. One of the employees of the printing shop followed them. This young man noticed the devotion of the English boy to the Church and made a systematic effort to turn him away. He would frequently say, "When you get as old as I am, George, you will see how false it is and will give it up."

One day he was boasting to his companions about an immoral escapade he had had the night before, not knowing that the boy was listening. When he finished, the small, slender lad walked up to him, shook his fist in his face and said: "D--- you, Tom Rolfe. You told me that when I grow up, I will lose my faith in this Church. I certainly will if I do the wicked things you're boasting about."

Instructor, April 1944, p. 161.

GEORGE Q. CANNON

"He Was Hungry Again"

The first winter the Saints spent in the valley was a remarkably mild one. There were two or three cold spells of weather but they did not last long. This was most fortunate for the people, for neither their food nor their clothing was of such a character as to enable them to endure very cold weather. . . .

The food had to be carefully husbanded. The greater part of the people weighed out their flour and cooked and ate so much each day. Those who were destitute had to be helped. . . . Bishops Tarleton Lewis and Edward Hunter were appointed to act in behalf of the destitute and to see that they did not suffer. In the spring, the thistle-tops were cooked for greens, and pronounced excellent.

Living on short rations was particularly hard on young people who were growing, and who had plenty of steady hard work to do. After living for months without having an opportunity of gratifying the appetite to its full extent, they would be apt to wonder how it was, when they had plenty of food, and the privilege of eating all they wished, they ever stopped eating; for in the hungry condition in which they were then, it seemed to them that if they had plenty of food they would not know how to stop eating it. Their systems, being reduced by the scantiness of their food, and the hard labor they had to perform, craved nourishment, and the filling of the stomach once did not satisfy this craving. We will relate an instance to illustrate this:

A boy who was approaching manhood was allowed the privilege of inviting some of his companions to dinner on his birthday, which happened to be in mid-winter, when the scarcity of food was probably felt more keenly than at the other time during the season of scarcity. At that meal, and for that occasion only, as it was his birthday, food was not to be measured, but all were to eat as much as they pleased. Some . . . may have had the experience of living for some time on a short allowance of food. If so, they can easily imagine the feeling of the boy whose birthday was to be thus celebrated. He dwelt with a rare anticipation of enjoyment on the feast in preparation, and made his calculations on the quantity he meant to eat. "I will eat," said he to himself, "enough at that meal to make up for the scantiness of many future meals." But alas! he found, when he had done his best, that he had eaten but little more than his usual rations, and had failed completely in laying up such a store as he had anticipated. He had not been aware until he made this trial, that his stomach had contracted, and had accommodated itself to the limited quantity of food which it received at each meal, and, therefore, could not be so suddenly distended for one meal to suit his wishes. Half an hour after he had eaten, he was hungry again.

Preston Nibley, *LDS Adventure Stories* (Bookcraft, 1953), pp. 93-105.

"I Felt a Peculiar Sensation in My Ears"

The white people were not numerous at Lahaina, and there were but very few at any other place on the island of Maui. Preaching to them with the hope of convincing them of the truth seemed a hopeless labor. The question arose directly, "Shall we confine our labors to the white people?" It is true that we had not been particularly told to preach to the natives of the islands, but we were in their midst, had full authority to declare unto them the message of salvation, and if we did not declare it unto them, some other Elders would have to come and do so, in order to fulfill the command of God to his servants.

For my part I felt it to be clearly my duty to warn all men, white and red; and no sooner did I learn the condition of the population than I made up my mind to acquire the language, preach the gospel to the natives and to the whites whenever I could obtain an opportunity, and thus fill my mission. I felt resolved to stay there, master the language and warn the people of those islands, if I had to do it alone; for I felt that I could not do otherwise and be free from condemnation; the spirit of it was upon me. Elders Bigler and Keeler felt the same. . . .

My desire to learn to speak was very strong; it was present with me night and day, and I never permitted an opportunity of talking with the natives to pass without improving it. I also tried to exercise faith before the Lord to obtain the gift of talking and understanding the language. One evening, while sitting on the mats conversing with some neighbors who had dropped in, I felt an uncommonly great desire to understand what they said. All at once I felt a peculiar sensation in my ears; I jumped to my feet, with my hands at the sides of my head, and exclaimed to Elders Bigler and Keeler who sat at the table, that I believed I had received the gift of interpretation! And it was so!

From that time forward I had but little, if any, difficulty in understanding what the people said. I might not be able at once to separate every word which they spoke from every other word in the sentence; but I could tell the general meaning of the whole. This was a great aid to me in learning to speak the language, and I felt very thankful for this gift from the Lord.

I mention this that my readers may know how willing God is to bestow gifts upon his children. If they should be called to go as missionaries to a foreign nation whose language they do not understand, it is their privilege to exercise faith for the gifts of speaking and interpreting that language, and also for every other gift which they may need.

(George Q. Cannon and four companions remained in the Hawaiian Islands four years and worked among the native people. At the end of 1853 they had baptized 4,000 natives and firmly established the Church in that land.)

Preston Nibley, *Missionary Experiences* (Deseret News Press, 1942), pp. 125-28.

GEORGE Q. CANNON

"I Took the 'Poi' in Preference to the Bread"

The principal food of the natives of the Sandwich Islands [Hawaii] is called *poi*. This is made out of a root which they call *kalo*. "Kalo" patches are so made that they can be flooded with water; and the ground is never allowed to be uncovered. In planting this root they do not use seed. When a native gathers the "kalo," he carries it to his home, where he cuts off the tops. These are carefully saved, tied up in a bundle, and carried back to the patch. These tops he sticks in the mud at the proper distances apart, and at the end of eleven months he has another crop of "kalo." This is the process of gathering and planting.

The "kalo" bears some resemblance in its leaves and taste to the wild Indian turnips, but its root is much larger; not quite the shape of a tame turnip, but as large as a moderate sized one. There is a variety called the "dry land kalo." It is not so extensively cultivated as the other kind, and is not considered so good eating.

When the "kalo" has been in long enough to cook, it is uncovered; the skin is washed off, and it is pounded with a stone pestle, on a large, flat slab of wood, until it is like a mass of dough. Then it is put into a calabash, or gourd, and by the next day fermentation has commenced; or, as we would say if it were bread, it has "raised." Water is then added to it, and it is mixed until it is a little thinner than we usually make mush. There is a little sour taste about it the first day. But it is never eaten at that time by the natives, unless they have no other food. They like it best when it is quite sour. This is what they call "poi," and there is no other food that they think can equal it.

Their usual method of eating is worthy of notice. A large calabash of "poi" is placed on the mats; around this the family seat themselves.

In families where they make any pretensions to cleanliness, a small calabash of water is passed around, and each one rinses his or her fingers before commencing to eat.

To keep off the flies, a boy or a girl stands waving a *kahili,* which is made by fastening feathers to a long, slender stick.

In eating, they dip their first two fingers into the calabash, load them with the "poi," and pass them into their mouths. The sucking of the fingers, the gusto with which they eat, and the incessant conversation mingled with laughter which they keep up, would lead a bystander to conclude that they enjoy their food. And they do. If the "poi" be good, and they have plenty of fish or meat to eat with it, they have great pleasure in eating. They think white men who eat together without conversing very unsocial beings. They have an idea that it contributes to health and to the enjoyment of the food to have pleasant and lively conversation while eating.

Before leaving Lahaina, I had tasted a teaspoonful of "poi"; but the smell of it and the calabash in which it was contained was so much like that of a bookbinder's old, sour, pastepot that when I put it to my mouth I gagged at it, and would have vomited had I swallowed it. But in traveling among the people I soon learned that if I did not eat "poi" I would put them to great inconvenience; for they would have to cook separate food for me every meal. This would make me burdensome to them, and might interfere with my success. I, therefore, determined to learn to live on their food, and, that I might do so, I asked the Lord to make it sweet to me. My prayer was heard and answered; the next time I tasted it, I ate a bowlful, and I positively liked it. It was my food, whenever I could get it from that time as long as I remained on the islands.

It may sound strange, yet it is true, that I have sat down to a table on which bread was placed, and though I had not tasted the latter for months, I took "poi" in preference to the bread; it was sweeter to me than any food I had ever eaten.

George Q. Cannon, "My First Mission," in Preston Nibley, comp., *Three Mormon Classics* (Bookcraft, 1944), pp. 144-47.

GEORGE Q. CANNON

"He Gave Us a Five-Dollar Gold Piece"

One incident, I will relate, which occurred a few months after we went to Wailuku, to show how the Lord hears and answers prayer.

We were very much in need of some means to buy stuff for garments, etc. The natives were very poor, and we felt delicate about asking them for anything; but we knew that the Lord would hear and answer our prayers; so we prayed to Him. Brother Hammond had brought his wife and child over from Lahaina. . . . He and I had to make a visit to a town about twelve or fifteen miles distant, and before starting, we had prayed to the Lord to open the way so that we might obtain what we wanted.

We had traveled from the house about three miles, when, in passing some houses which were on the beach, we met a man by the name of Freeman, an American, who accosted us and inquired if we had authority to marry. Upon our informing him that we had, he asked us if we could spare the time to stop at his house and marry him. We told him as it was on our way we would stop. I performed the ceremony, and at his request addressed the people who had assembled at the house. He gave us a five-dollar gold piece.

We had married many before that, but this was the first money which had ever been given to us. His five dollars supplied our necessities, for in those days we were content with very little.

I have always looked upon this as a direct answer to our prayers, for when we met the man he was evidently on his way to Wailuku, with his intended wife, to be married by the missionary there. The missionary missed the fee, but as he knew nothing respecting it, he was no poorer. I do not suppose he needed it as badly as we did.

It is always more pleasant for an Elder, when he is in need of anything, on a mission, to apply to the Lord for it than to ask the people; at least, I have always found it so.

Nibley, *Three Mormon Classics* (Bookcraft), pp. 180-81.

"Never Were Men Happier"

The Lord had revealed unto me that it was my duty to remain on the islands, acquire the language, and bear testimony of His great work to the people. He had given me many promises connected therewith. And now I began to feel how true His words had been. Many and many a time, when I sat in the meetings and heard the people speak in the demonstration of the Spirit of the Lord, filled with its power and its holy influence, bearing testimony to the truth of the gospel, to its restoration and to the gifts which had been bestowed, my joy was so great that I could scarcely contain myself. I felt that, however devotedly I might labor, I could not show the gratitude to the Lord which I felt, at being permitted to receive the Priesthood and to exercise it for the salvation of the children of men. Surely, never were men happier than we who labored in the ministry among that people in those days; we had a fullness of joy, and it seemed as if there were no room for more.

The people, too, with all their faults and weaknesses, were greatly blessed. The power of God rested mightily upon them, and many a time their faces would glisten and appear almost white under the influence of the Spirit. They knew that Jesus was the Son of God and the Savior of the world, and that Joseph Smith and Brigham Young were Prophets and servants of God. This knowledge had come to them through obedience to the commandments.

Nibley, *Three Mormon Classics* (Bookcraft), pp. 169-70.

"The Pangs of Parting"

In the spring of 1854, word came from the brethren in Salt Lake City that George and his four original companions were free to return home. They continued to labor until July of that year, when at last he prepared to board the ship at Honolulu. The Elders would not have been able to return even then had it not been for the generosity of the Saints, who raised enough money to help pay for their passage. When they arrived at the wharf, they were greeted by hundreds of Saints who were gathered to bid them farewell. These Saints had prepared a huge feast in their honor and planned to have a two-day farewell meeting. Not only had the Saints gathered, but there were also many non-members of the Church, government officials and others who had known and learned to love Elder Cannon. Typical of his humility, he recognized his fame without taking credit for it. He knew the source and purpose of it:

During my travels on the different islands I have been surprised at my own notoriety. They seemed to be as well acquainted with me on Kauai as far as my name (Geogi Pukuniahi) and my proceedings were concerned, as they were on Maui. As far as a name is concerned I have got one on these lands, and the Lord has blessed me with influence far beyond what I ever could have expected, but I do not want the praise of men. I desire to be approved by my Heavenly Father and all the influence I can attain to over the hearts of the children of men I desire to have wisdom and grace to use it in spreading and building the kingdom of God.

Elder Cannon recorded that night the feelings he had as he sat before the table laden with the sumptuous feast these native people of modest means had prepared in his honor.

I could not eat, all my appetite had left me, the thoughts of leaving those with whom I had been associated in all circumstances for years on the closest terms of brotherly intimacy, deprived me of all relish for food; my feelings were poignant, and the pangs of parting deprived me of all feelings of joy at the prospect that was opening before me of seeing my mountain home with all its loved associations.

As the ship bearing the Elders set sail for San Francisco, Elder Cannon watched the islands fade into the distance. Only a few years before, the message of the restoration had not been heard on these islands, and now there were "upwards of four thousand members of the Church in Hawaii." He could not help but compare the difference between their modest arrival and this glorious send-off:

How great the contrast between our landing and our departure! We had landed there friendless and unknown—so far as man was concerned. Now there were thousands who loved us, who rejoiced in the truth of the gospel and in the testimony of Jesus. On that wharf that day was an illustration of the wonderful power of the gospel in creating love in the hearts of the children of men. We had gone forth weeping and bearing precious seed. The Lord had given us souls for our hire.

---

[1]Flake, *George Q. Cannon: His Missionary Years*, pp. 98-100.

GEORGE Q. CANNON

"I Knew I Had But to Call"

In early April, President Young called upon George Q. Cannon to perform another publishing mission. He was to remove the press and type and some supplies of the *Deseret News* to Fillmore, Utah, and publish the paper there, reducing it in size from eight to four pages.

Elder Cannon continued to publish the *News* until early September when he was directed to return the press to Great

Salt Lake City. When he reached Payson with his heavily loaded wagons, a messenger from President Young met him with some very unexpected news. If he had any dreams of finally being able to settle down to a "normal" life, they would have to wait. The message contained another mission call, this time to the Eastern Sates. Elder Cannon recalled this incident in these words:

> At Payson at noon on Monday, as I was unhitching my team at Brother William B. Preston's . . . Brother John Bollwinkle drove up with a carriage and mules and handed me a note. It was from President Young, and was dated the previous Sunday. He informed me that I had been appointed to go East on a mission. The company I was to go with expected to start the next day (the day I received the note), and he wished me to come to the city as quickly as I could. In reply to my inquiry, the messenger said he would be ready to start back as soon as he had eaten his dinner and fed his mules.

> While he was gone, I gathered up what clothing and bedding and weapons I needed for the journey, and in about three quarters of an hour we were on our way to Salt Lake City, where we arrived the next morning as day was breaking.

He journeyed all night and reported to President Young early the next morning. Upon seeing him, Brigham Young turned to the others in the office and said, "Didn't I tell you it would be so? I knew I had but to call and here he is!"

Later on that same day, Elder Cannon was on his way to the East:

As I had only been home from a mission, a few weeks before I went to Fillmore, and had been absent several years before on another mission, I had no home in Salt Lake City. In leaving my family at the roadside, therefore, I left them with no bright prospect for comfort and ease during my absence. But they uttered no complaints. They put their trust in the Lord and during the two years of my absence, He was their benefactor and friend.

Flake, *George Q. Cannon: His Missionary Years,* pp. 141-42, 145-47.

"A Glorious Personage Appeared"

On my return from my visit to the east I took the opportunity of calling at Richmond, Ray County, Missouri, to see the last surviving witness of the three to whom the angel exhibited the plates of the Book of Mormon—David Whitmer.

From Kansas City I took train for Lexington Junction, and there changed cars for Richmond. Upon arriving at the station I inquired of a gentleman who was standing there if he knew Mr. Whitmer. He told me that his son, David J. Whitmer, would be there presently, as he owned the omnibus which carried passengers from the station to the hotels. In a short time the omnibus drove up, and the gentleman of whom I had made the inquiry pointed Mr. Whitmer out to me. I found him very courteous, and upon informing him who I was he appeared to have been expecting me, having heard through some of the papers that I was intending to make such a visit. He said his father was growing very feeble and he did not like to have him interviewed, but he would arrange for me to see him as soon as he could.

I drove to the hotel, and after dinner Mr. Whitmer called upon me and conducted me to the residence of his father. On our way there he pointed out the track of a cyclone which had visited the town in 1878, and which had left their house, or rather the room in which the manuscript of the Book of Mormon was kept, in such a condition as to astonish all the people. The roof of the house was blown off; but nothing in this room was disturbed. The glass was not even broken. This was a cause of astonishment to the neighborhood, and the family evidently ascribe the protection of the room and its contents to the fact of the manuscript being there.

David Whitmer, who was born in January, 1805, is growing feeble, but his mind is bright and apparently unimpaired. He is rather slender now and probably stood in his early manhood five feet ten or perhaps five feet eleven inches in height. I noticed in shaking hands with him that the thumb of his right hand is missing and the hand has a long scar in the center from some injury that he had received. His hair is thin and he is rather bald. His nose is aquiline; his eyes black, or a dark brown. I noticed a slight German accent or tone in his talk. The Whitmer family is of German origin, his mother, I believe, having been born on the Rhine. He has evidently been a man who in his prime must have been quite interesting, and, I should think, fine looking. I was shown a likeness of his, painted in oil, when he was thirty-two years old. This makes him appear as handsome, of marked features, rather Jewish looking, with a head of thick hair inclined to curl.

After some little conversation he inquired of me if I would like to see the manuscript, and gave his son a key and told him to bring it in. I found it wonderfully well preserved, written in different handwritings. He says they are the writings of Oliver Cowdery, Emma Smith, Martin Harris, and perhaps, some of it that of his brother Christian, who assisted the Prophet Joseph. This is the manuscript, Mr. Whitmer says, from which the printers set the type of the Book of Mormon, and he pointed out to me where it had been cut for conveniences as "copy." I noticed some printer's marks on the manuscript. Still it seemed unusually clean for "copy" that printers had handled. I commented upon the cleanness of the manuscript and he explained that it was in consequence of the care taken of it by Oliver Cowdery in watching it while in the printer's hands. It was fastened together not as a whole, but a few sheets—probably not more than a dozen—with woolen yarn, which he said was his mother's. I examined this manuscript with great interest and with a feeling of reverence. How many associations cluster around this! What wonderful changes have occurred since the few who were interested in this work labored in its preparation under the direction of the Prophet! Everything connected with the work then was in the future. Their minds were filled with anticipation concerning the greatness of the work the foundation of which they were assisting. Thoughts like this passed through my mind while looking at this manuscript.

But there was a paper with this, which, if anything, was still more interesting than the manuscript. It was the characters drawn by Joseph himself from the plates for Martin Harris to take to show the learned professors, so wonderfully predicted in the 29th chapter of Isaiah. There were seven lines of these characters, the first four being about twice as large in size as the last three. In English Joseph had written over the lines the word "characters." He had spelled this word, "caractors." Though these characters had evidently been written for a long time, they were as clear and distinct as though just penned. Here was the very paper which Isaiah saw in vision about 2,600 years before, and which he called "the words of a book." How wonderfully God in His own way brings to pass the fulfillment of the predictions of his servants! To the ordinary person it might seem like a trifling thing to copy these characters and send them "to one that is learned"; but it was of sufficient importance in the mind of the Lord for him to inspire his servant Isaiah to describe exactly the occurrence. This shows how much importance the Lord attached to these details connected with the foundation of this work and the coming forth of the Book of Mormon.

David Whitmer told me he was plowing when Joseph and Oliver came to him to speak about his being one of the witnesses. He already knew that the Lord had promised to show the plates to three witnesses. Joseph then informed him that he was chosen to be one of the three. They went out and sat upon a log, conversing upon the things to be revealed, when they were surrounded by a glorious light which overshadowed them. A glorious personage appeared unto them and exhibited to them the plates, the sword of Laban, the Directors which were given to Lehi (called Liahona), the Urim and Thummim, and other records. Human language cannot, he said, describe what they saw. He had had his hours of darkness and trial and difficulty since that period; but however dark upon other things his mind had been, that vision had ever been a bright and beautiful scene in his memory, and he had never wavered in regard to it. He had fearlessly testified of it always, even when his life was threatened. Martin Harris was not with them at the time Joseph and Oliver and he saw the angel; but he and Joseph afterwards were together, and the angel exhibited the plates to Martin Harris also, and he thus became a witness.

I spent several hours there, and to me they were very interesting. The old gentleman was able to stay in the room only a portion of the time; he had to retire to rest; but I had the company of his son, David J. Whitmer, and his nephew, John C. Whitmer (who is a son of Jacob Whitmer, one of the eight witnesses to the Book of Mormon), while I remained.

Nibley, *L. D. S. Adventure Stories* (Bookcraft), pp. 93-97.

GEORGE Q. CANNON

"Charles Dickens"

More than 13,000 were emigrated under President Cannon's direction. The port of departure was Liverpool, but on a few occasions ships were sent out from London. The first of these was the *Amazon* with nearly nine hundred Saints aboard. The sailing was June 4, 1863. This is the ship visited by Charles Dickens, and he tells of it in his *Uncommercial Traveler*. The agent was George Q. Cannon. We quote some passages from that interesting account:

"Now, I have seen emigrant ships before this day in June, and these people are so strikingly different from all other people in like circumstances. . . .

". . . nobody in ill-temper, nobody is the worse for drink, nobody swears an oath or uses a coarse word, nobody appears depressed, nobody is weeping. . . ."

Then Dickens quotes what the captain of the ship says about them. "Most of these came aboard yesterday evening. They came from various parts of England, in small parties that had never seen one another before. Yet they had not been a couple of hours on board when they had established their own police, made their own regulations, and set their own watches at all the hatchways. Before nine o'clock the ship was as orderly and as quiet as a man-o-war.

"The Mormon agent who had been active in getting them together, and in making the contract with my friends the owners of the ship to take them as far as New York on their way to the Great Salt Lake, was pointed out to me. A compactly-made handsome man in black, rather short, with rich brown hair and beard, and clear bright eyes. From his speech, I should set him down as American, probably a man who had 'knocked about the world' pretty much. A man with a frank, open manner, and unshrinking look; withal a man of great quickness."

In the conversation with Elder Cannon, Dickens, the uncommercial Traveler, remarks: "I think it would be difficult to find eight hundred people together anywhere else, and find so much beauty and so much strength and capacity for work among them. . . .

"I went on board their ship to bear testimony against them if they deserved it, as I fully believed they would; to my great astonishment they did not deserve it; and my predispositions and tendencies must not affect me as an honest witness. I went over the Amazon's side, feeling it impossible to deny that, so far, some remarkable influence had produced remarkable result, which better known influences have often missed."

Instructor, January 1945, p. 12-13.

Biographical Sketch

ELDER RUDGER CLAWSON

As a tribute to President Clawson on his 80th birthday, Bryant S. Hinkley wrote the following:

Rudger Clawson stands upon the summit of eighty years, a quiet, fearless defender of the faith; a God-fearing, benevolent leader of men.

What more fitting tribute could be paid to a man who spent the greater part of his life in the service of his God.

Rudger Clawson was born on March 12, 1857, in Salt Lake City, Utah, to Bishop Hiram B. Clawson and Mary Gay Judd Clawson. He was born at a very trying time for his pioneer parents, just preceding the Utah War. Among his early associates were young men like Heber J. Grant, Abraham H. Cannon, Orson F. Whitney, and others.

At the age of eighteen he became the private secretary to John W. Young, the president of Utah Western Railway, and in this capacity traveled to New York City for a period of two years. Early in his educational career he became skilled as an accountant and businessman. Shortly after his return from New York, Rudger was called on a mission to the Southern States.

On February 5, 1888, Elder Clawson was called to be the president of the Box Elder Stake in Brigham City, Utah. On

October 10, 1898, he was ordained an apostle by Lorenzo Snow and became a member of the Quorum of the Twelve.

He presided over the European Mission for three years (1910-13).

Elder Clawson was President of the Quorum of the Twelve from 1921 until his death June 21, 1943.

Richard L. Evans wrote the following about President Clawson in March of 1942 after President Clawson had been leading the Council of the Twelve for over twenty years.

From his youth in a favored home, guided by noble parents, until this present eminence of years, he has walked the ways of life in goodness with quiet effectiveness, and with full regard for the demands of duty.

RUDGER CLAWSON

"The Death of Joseph Standing"

The account of Joseph Standing's martyrdom which follows is substantially as related by President Clawson to the writer.[1]

As these missionaries made their way on foot to the conference Elder Standing related a dream he had had which greatly impressed him and which was weighing heavily upon his mind. The dream proved to be a premonition of the awful tragedy here related.

After a long and tiresome day's journey, near midnight, the Elders knocked at the door of Mr. Holston, not a member of the Church. After explaining to him who they were he said: "Gentlemen, come in. You are welcome to my home." He secured a light and said further: "In all likelihood the mob will be here searching for you—but," said he with clenched fists and great emphasis, "if they come into my yard I will shoot them down like dogs." He knew what a mob meant but he was unafraid. The Elders were shown to their room. Fatigued with the journey and exhausted with anxiety they were soon lost in

---

[1]The writer is Bryant S. Hinckley.

sleep. The morning of July 21, 1879, dawned bright and beautiful. It was Sunday—peace permeated the very atmosphere they breathed. There was a calmness and a spirit of tranquillity that was in keeping with the Holy day; it was, however, but the calm that precedes the cyclone.

After expressing their gratitude and appreciation to Mr. Holston and explaining that they would call on their way back, the young missionaries started on their journey. Peace was in their youthful hearts. They carried the message of good will toward all men. They were young, alone, unarmed, and far from home. Their only armor of defense was the truth. As they walked through the primeval woods of Georgia with the feeling that all the trouble was over, they made a turn in the road and suddenly came in view of an armed mob.

With shouts and vile imprecations the mob charged down upon them. The leader said: "You are our prisoners." Elder Standing replied: "By what authority do you arrest us upon the public highway? If you have a warrant for our arrest we should like to see it." The answer was: "The United States of America is 'agin' you and there is no law in Georgia for the Mormons. You go with us." "We'll show you by what authority we act!" some of them shouted.

The mobocrats led the way and the missionaries followed. Elder Standing was greatly agitated. He was deathly pale and moved nervously and quickly all the time, endeavoring to explain to the mob the nature of their mission, what they were doing—expostulating with them to no avail. Elder Clawson walked more deliberately and slowly, which seemed to exasperate one of the fiends behind him who gave him a heavy blow on the back of the head which almost felled him to the ground. A few minutes later this same murderer raised a heavy club and was about to deliver a death-dealing blow to this innocent man when one of the mob caught his arm. This vicious fellow had already flourished a cocked pistol menacingly in Elder Clawson's face accompanied with oaths and threats.

As they went along Elder Standing repeatedly asked for water. He seemed to have an insatiable thirst. They soon reached a spring of water in a secluded spot deep in the woods.

58

They sat around this spring and one of the mobocrats said to Elder Standing: "There's the water; you've been asking for it; why don't you drink?" Elder Standing said: "I don't wish to drink now." "You needn't be afraid; we won't hurt you while you do." There upon Elder Standing walked slowly to the spring, lay down and drank and drank. It seemed almost impossible for him to quench his thirst. He returned to his seat in the circle. A desultory conversation ensued in the course of which the vilest accusations were laid against the Mormons. A space of nearly an hour was consumed in this way.

We quote the words of President Clawson:

The fateful moment had arrived. The three men on horses rode up. The presumption is that they had left the party shortly after our arrest for the purpose of locating a secluded place in the forest to carry out the intent of the mob. . . . The spokesman with a rifle in his trembling hands, for he appeared greatly agitated, said: "Follow us." . . . At that critical instant, Joseph Standing jumped to his feet, turned and faced the horsemen, clasped his hands firmly together, and said in a commanding voice, "Surrender."

As the word "Surrender" left the lips of Joseph Standing, one of the men sitting in the circle pointed his weapon at Elder Standing and fired. Elder Standing, whirling in his tracks, fell heavily to the ground face downward, and immediately turned upon his back with his face upward. The mobocrats instantly stood upon their feet. A cloud of smoke and dust enveloped the body of the wounded man. At this critical juncture the leading mobocrat, pointing at me, said: "Shoot that man." Every weapon was leveled at my head. My time had come, so it seemed to me. My turn to follow Joseph Standing was at hand. The command to shoot had been given. I was looking down the gun barrels of the murderous mobs. I folded my arms and said: "Shoot," and almost persuaded myself that I was shot, so intense were my feelings.

I quickly recovered my presence of mind when I heard the voice of a mobocrat which said hurriedly and in a tone of fear: "Don't shoot."

I then stepped over to the spot where Joseph Standing had fallen. He was breathing heavily; the death rattle was in his throat and a great, gaping bullet wound appeared in his forehead just above the bridge of his nose. He was unconscious. I did not speak to him. I saw at a glance that he was beyond all earthly help.

The chief mobocrat stepped up by my side and together we stood looking down upon the prostrate form of the dying man. Do you ask, "What does one experience who receives a bullet into his body at a vital point?" I can tell you, although no bullet has ever entered my body. When the guns and pistols of the mobocrats were leveled at my head and the command to fire had been given, I thought I was actually shot and suffered for a moment or two the agony of a dying man. With my eyes wide open, gazing into the muzzles of the deadly weapons, instantly the sight went out of my eyes; total blindness followed, and I was enveloped in darkness. The world around me seemed to be blotted out. When I heard the voice in command say: "Don't shoot," it was just then that the realization came to me that I had not been shot. My sight gradually returned and I lived again, so to speak.

I am sure this was the experience of Elder Standing, only in his case he did not live again.

Suddenly the mob appeared to sense the horrible character of the deed they had committed, and seized with consternation they instinctively rushed together in a compact group as if seeking mutual protection. Elder Clawson walked over to where Elder Standing was lying, stooped and looked into his face. He was breathing heavily. He raised the dying man's head, and tenderly placed his hat under it to keep it out of the dust. An awful sense of grief and utter loneliness seized him; he could only put his trust in God. He exclaimed: "Gentlemen, it is a burning shame to leave a man to die in these woods this way. For Heaven's sake, either you go and secure assistance that the body may be removed and cared for or allow me to do so." After a moment's consultation they said: "You go."

Elder Clawson set out at once to find the coroner. It took him from ten o'clock in the morning until sunset to get the coroner and his assistant to the place where the body lay. He says: "I was horrified to discover that the mob had returned— presumably while Elder Standing was yet alive—and had fired several shots into his face and neck." The coroner's jury, after due deliberation, rendered a verdict to the effect that Joseph Standing met his death from gun shots fired by a mob—giving their names. The body was then released.

A door was secured from a deserted cabin near by, the body placed upon it, and six men, Brother Clawson being one of them, carried the remains to Mr. Holston's home where it was placed on a scaffold out under the trees. It was now well into the night. The coroner before leaving said: "Mr. Clawson, why don't you bury the body here in Georgia? After some years you can take up the bones and move them to Utah." He said,

"Never, never, never! I am going to do for my companion what he would do for me under like circumstances. I tell you frankly, Mr. Coroner, if I had been shot to death in Georgia, as he was shot to death, I would not wish to be buried in this soil. I am sure Joseph Standing feels that way, I am going to take his body home." "Well," said the coroner, "you will not be able to do it."

Quoting from Brother Clawson:

It became my duty to prepare the body. I had never before touched a dead person, and yet there was no help for it. Under the feeble light of several candles I washed the body. With painstaking care I washed the wounds. To me it was a painful ordeal—but willingly and tenderly performed.

It was far into the dark before he completed this sad and difficult service. This was a supreme test of his loyalty to his companion. All who read this story must know that Rudger Clawson in a supreme and crucial hour displayed the spirit and courage of a martyr.

He proceeded to secure the best metallic casket obtainable—placed the body in it and had it carefully sealed. However, almost insurmountable difficulties were experienced before the railroad would receive the body for shipment. He was forced to place the metallic casket in a large wooden box and surround it with dry cinders. It was then carried by rail from Dalton, Georgia, to Salt Lake City, a distance of three thousand miles.

Improvement Era, March 1937, pp. 135-37.

Biographical Sketch

Elder Cowley was born on August 2, 1897, at Preston, Idaho, the son of Matthias F. Cowley and Abbie Hyde. He was called to serve a mission in New Zealand when just seventeen years old.

He received a law degree from George Washington University.

In 1938 Elder Cowley was called to preside over the New Zealand Mission.

On July 13, 1922, while still studying in Washington, D.C., he returned home to be married in the Salt Lake Temple to Elva Eleanor Taylor. Their marriage was performed by President George Albert Smith, then a member of the Council of the Twelve.

On October 5, 1945, Brother Cowley was sustained a member of the Council of the Twelve as the Church met in solemn assembly in its semiannual conference. In this conference, President George Albert Smith was sustained as the President of the Church, and his first call to the apostleship went to this young man whom he had guided and loved since early childhood.

On October 11, 1945, Elder Cowley was ordained an apostle, the sixty-fifth of this dispensation, by President Smith. Approximately a year later, a new position of responsibility among the General Authorities of the Church was created, and Elder Cowley was appointed to fill the position as president of the Pacific Islands missions. In this new assignment, he was given the responsibility of directing the affairs of the Church in the many missions of the Pacific. His headquarters in this assignment continued to be in Salt Lake City, but during the following three years, he traveled almost continuously in the islands of the sea. The entire Polynesian people now had the opportunity of being blessed by him as had the Maori people during the years that he had lived with them as missionary and president.

He had a great gift of language and was able to speak in the native tongue so that he could be understood by the people in all his travels. In addition to his travels in the islands, he visited in the missions of the Orient and in Australia. He visited the Philippine Islands, Japan, and China, dedicating China once again for the preaching of the gospel. After approximately three years in this special assignment, he was released, and from then until his death, he traveled extensively along with the other General Authorities, visiting the stakes and the missions of the Church.

At the time of his passing on December 13, 1953, he had become one of the most loved men of his time. Few men have ever been so greatly loved and so greatly respected. He affected the lives of everyone who knew him.

Matthew Cowley Speaks (Deseret Book Co., 1971), pp. vii-xii.

MATTHEW COWLEY

"Seventeen Years of Age"

How I remember as a mere boy —I was alone for three months without a companion, not understanding the native language—how I would go into the grove every morning at six o'clock and study for eleven hours and fast and pray. Finally, within eleven or twelve weeks and all by myself with no missionary to encourage me, I had the audacity to stand up before a group of natives and preach the gospel in their own tongue. I was using words I had never read or heard, and there was a burning in my bosom the like of which I have never felt before nor since in my life. My mind was not like I was a child. The power of God was speaking through me as a youngster, seventeen years of age.

Henry A. Smith, *Matthew Cowley—Man of Faith* (Bookcraft, 1954), p. 48.

"My Family Were on Their Knees"

I want to tell you, brothers and sisters, that I have prayed so many times and so much during the last few months that almost unconsciously I have caught myself getting down to pray right on the street. The integrity of the Mormon home is founded on prayer in the family circle. The Holy of Holies in this Church is not in this tabernacle or in the temple, but it is in your home. That is where you are testing the saving powers of the gospel of Jesus Christ. How I used to appreciate my father when I was away at school or out in the islands doing missionary work. For eight months I was very sick. I had boils, sunstroke, tapeworms, was kicked in the abdomen by a horse, and it was just one thing after another. I used to wake up in the morning, and I would say to myself, "Well, all of them at home, my father, mother, and brothers and sisters are down on their knees offering up their prayers in my behalf." And when the dusk would come and night would fall, I would know that over 8,000 miles away my family were on their knees offering up their prayers, and that in their prayers my name was being mentioned. That meant something to me. I thank God that the integrity of my home was never broken— my father's home. Even after I was married and went to my father's home, before I got out of the door, he would say, "Come back here, I am still the patriarch of this family, and you are entitled to my blessing," and he would pray. He poured out his soul to God, but all the time he was preaching the gospel to me through prayer.

Matthew Cowley Speaks, p. 162.

"That Morning We Met at the Temple"

I was struggling to earn my way in Washington, to get an education, and I didn't have enough money to come and get married in the temple. We even had the announcements printed, and then all of a sudden my father heard about it. . . . He wasn't a man of means. He was never successful in a business way, and I guess things looked pretty dark for him as far as I was concerned. So he went out and put his hand into the hand of God. I know he did it on his knees, and in response to that prayer, I received money from him, and he said, "You have to come home and get married right in the first instance."

I came home, and we went to the temple. It was the 13th of July. That morning we met at the temple, my father and my mother, and some others of our family. We came around from West Temple where we lived, just across the street from Temple Square. My wife and her family came together, and we met at the little gate in the east wall of the temple.

Smith, *Matthew Cowley—Man of Faith* (Bookcraft), p. 82.

"These Natives Live Close to God"

He [Matthew Cowley] should have been somewhat prepared for the call to the apostleship that came to him. . . . Had not his native friends predicted this assignment for him? One particular instance which he must have remembered occurred in New Zealand when the Saints of the mission were gathered in a memorial service for Elder Rufus K. Hardy. One native speaker was lamenting the mission's serious loss in Elder Hardy's being taken from the Presiding Councils of the Church when he suddenly stopped, looked at President Cowley and said:

"Wait a minute. There's nothing to worry about. When President Cowley gets home, he'll fill the first vacancy in the Council of the Twelve Apostles, and we'll still have a representative among the Authorities of the Church."

Tumuaki Cowley knew that his could not have been a chance remark. Too often before had he witnessed the inspiration of the Lord come to these people. "These natives live close to God. They have some kind of power. I guess it's just because they accept miracles as a matter of course. They never doubt anything," he said of them.

Smith, *Matthew Cowley—Man of Faith* (Bookcraft), p. 152.

"Elder Cowley—1947"

Elder Cowley arrived at the Samoan Islands Wednesday July 2, 1947. A reception was held by the saints in behalf of Elder Cowley's arrival. President John Adams, of the Samoan Mission, reported as Elder Cowley arrived, "The greeting was spontaneous and warm." . . . "The older men, and some women crossed to the large Samoan style building on the Chapel lot, where the impressive island ceremony of passing the native drink of respect, Ava, with accompanying speeches from both sides, was done in royal fashion. All were impressed and delighted with Elder Cowley's spirit and response and congenial handling of his part."

Some of the natives had erected a large sign for the welcome of Elder Cowley. They had printed on the sign "Angel Moroni-1823; Elder Cowley-1947" with a big WELCOME in-between. The Church leader asked the significance of the sign and they pointed skyward from whence Elder Cowley had just arrived by airplane and explained that both the Angel Moroni and Elder Cowley had come from the heavens to bring them the truths of the everlasting gospel.

Church News, August 2, 1947, p. 8; August 16, 1947, p. 7.

"A Hundred and Ten Live Pigs"

I love this work, my brothers and sisters. I thank God for my missionary companions. The traveling which I do is sometimes hazardous, but I love it; I feel the protection of the Almighty God.

We left New Zealand three or four weeks ago, and I was on one of those fine clippers of the air. Two hours out of New Zealand we struck a violent storm. The first thing I realized was that we had struck something. As a matter of fact, we had been struck by lightning. The lightning had penetrated the nose of the ship, and that lightning ball bounced around the plane. How it missed the propellers, I do not know. It destroyed one stabilizer on the plane. We continued on our way. I believe from that moment until we landed at Nandi, Fiji, God was the pilot of that plane, and I was his servant, praying that we might be landed safely at our destination.

I had no fear in my heart. I know that God looks after his own.

I was on a little ship in Tahiti, a little submarine chaser of about fifty tons, a converted submarine chaser. The way that thing acted I am sure it had not been converted; not properly so. Eight days I was on that submarine chaser, and there was never a calm moment. There were a hundred and ten live pigs on the deck space, and they were closed in by crates containing chickens. I think Tahiti is the only place in the world where roosters crow all night. And then just ahead in front of these porcine quadrupeds and the fowl, were thirty-eight seasick natives.

President Mitchell and I were in a tiny cabin. That ship tossed and rolled. We never had our clothes off for six days. I had to lie on my bunk and hang on to some pipes overhead to keep from being catapulted out into whatever space there was there, and I have never heard such a symphony in my life. I will never forget it. Pigs squealing, roosters crowing, sick natives, retching, and me hanging on for dear life. But I was not seasick. Never have I been seasick or plane sick or car sick or train sick. I have been sick, but it was never been caused by vehicles of transportation.

I left Tahiti in a freight ship. I was a member of the crew of that freight ship. It was the only way I could get on the ship. I had to go to the captain and ask him if he would take me on as a passenger, and he said: "No, we are not allowed to take passengers."

I said: "May I sign on as a member of the crew?"

He said: "I think that can be arranged."

And so I signed on as a member of the crew, and I went from there to New Zealand. I never did find out what my duties were on that ship as a member of the crew. I thought for a time that I might be the chaplain, but we crossed the international date line Saturday night, and when I woke up it was Monday, so Sunday was scratched right out, and I could not even perform my duties as a chaplain.

When we arrived at Samoa, I was called to the bridge of the ship. The captain said to me: "Do you know where Apia, Samoa, is?"

I said: "Yes, you are just passing it."

He had passed our port of destination, so we turned back and went into Apia. From there, we went on to New Zealand, and before they started doing the heavy work of unloading the ship, I signed off as a member of the crew.

God opens up the way, brothers and sisters, for his servants to accomplish their work.

Smith, *Matthew Cowley—Man of Faith* (Bookcraft), pp. 140-41, 152.

"The Market Price"

I would like to add a story or two here to those which have been related by Bishop Richards. Down in Tahiti where I have recently visited . . . our people there have a seasonal occupation of pearl shell diving, and our men are the best shell divers in the islands of French Oceania. Why are they the best divers? Because they keep the Word of Wisdom, and they can stay under the water longer than the others who do not. They stay under the water at a depth of ninety feet for upwards of two minutes and forty seconds. They dive to that depth and bring up the pearl shell which gives them part of their means of support for the remainder of the year until the next season approaches.

This one young Latter-day Saint placed his pearl shells on the shore in two piles, one was a large one and one a rather small one, and when the trader came around with whom he had the contract to sell his pearl shells, the trader asked him about the small pile. He said: "Is that yours?" He said: "No, that is not mine."

The trader said: "Where did it come from?"

He said: "Oh, I dove for it."

"Well, why is it not yours?"

He said: "That is God's pearl shell."

"Who has the right to sell it?"

He said: "I can sell it."

"Well, then, I will buy it."

"Yes, you may buy it, but not at the contract price. You will have to pay the market price for God's pearl shell"; because the market price had gone up since he had signed the contract.

And so he sold God's pearl shell at the market price and his own at the price for which he had contracted. And when I inquired what he would have done had the price gone down instead of up, he said: "I would have left it with mine. I would always see to it that God gets the top price for his pearl shell."

Matthew Cowley Speaks, pp. 5-6.

MATTHEW COWLEY

"Look in the Same Direction"

I was in a home recently in one of our stakes where a man was lying upon his bed. The only parts of his body that he could move were his eyes and his tongue. He could speak and he could see, but that was all; no life in his arms, no life in his legs. The home was immaculate; his bed linen was immaculate; he was immaculate. Maybe there was no life in his hand, but his companion held that hand in a grasp as strong as life itself. The clasp of the hand, brothers and sisters—it has meaning! And when you are away from one another, if you don't feel a spiritual clasp stronger than the physical clasp, rush back to one another as quickly as you can. You know true love is not looking at each other in one of those old-fashioned loveseats—looking into each other's eyes. That isn't true love. True love is that love which comes into your heart and motivates your life when you arise from the altar and both of you look in the same direction, down through eternity. That is true love, where both are looking in the same direction.

The Maori in referring to his wife says: "Taku hoa wahine."
That means, "My companion wife." The wife, in speaking

of her companion, says: "Taku hoa tane." "My companion husband." I like that a little better than just saying "My wife," or "My husband." "My companion wife," "My companion husband!" Companionship implies a oneness of direction, right down through eternity.

Matthew Cowley Speaks, pp. 13-14.

MATTHEW COWLEY

"He Was Always Holding Hands With His Wife"

Thank you, President McKay, for that beautiful picture of you and your wife, side by side, touching each other's hands in the room where your sainted mother was born.

When I went to New Zealand as mission president, I went around among the people. Those natives have great memories. They would quote from the sermons of mission presidents, but there had been one president out there whom they did not quote, but he preached to those people the most beautiful sermon they had ever witnessed. Wherever I would go and we would refer to that grand man, the natives would say, "He was always holding hands with his wife." When they would sit down together at the table, their hands would just naturally go toward each other, and they would hold hands—the greatest sermon that was ever delivered in the history of the New Zealand Mission, the sacred clasp of the hands of man and woman.

Matthew Cowley Speaks, pp. 14-15.

"My, Wouldn't That Be Wonderful"

He [God] is a wonderful partner, isn't he? He is wonderful. My, how I would like to have a partner like him in life. I would like to be in business with somebody like him, have my partner come up to me and say, "Here, I'll furnish all the capital to start the business. I will furnish all the blessings. Then, you look after the business. Don't forget me. When the increase comes, you keep ninety percent, turn over to me ten percent. You use your ninety percent any way you want to, and I'll put my ten percent right back into the business." My, wouldn't that be wonderful? That's just the kind of partner we have in this Church. We keep the ninety percent and use it anyway we wish, sometimes to our destruction. We give him the ten percent, and here stands a temple; here stands a tabernacle. He puts it all right back into the business, into his business. God will finance this Church, brothers and sisters, if you will obey the principles of the gospel.

Matthew Cowley Speaks, p. 77.

"That's Just Silly"

You know, I had an experience out in one part of the state here. I couldn't stay in the stake president's home because of sickness, and so the president of the Relief Society insisted that I go to her home. I thought that was wonderful. The lovely-looking Relief Society president and I went to her home, and we went inside. There sat a fine-looking man at the table playing a game with his children. I had never met him. His wife took me over and introduced me. She said, "You know, there is only one thing wrong with my husband." I said, "What is that?" She said, "He doesn't belong to the Church." So I said to him, "Hey, what's the idea? You're not supposed to be having home night with your children! That is our program. You don't belong to the Church. You are not supposed to be doing that." I was just kidding him along, you know. We got in quite a conversation. He said, "You know, I can't question the doctrine of your Church. Oh, I have studied it, and I have read the Bible, and I can't argue against the doctrine of your Church. It is right. But I go to fast meetings sometimes, and of all the silly, ridiculous things I ever heard in my life, are the fast meetings of the Mormon Church." I said, "What's that?" He said, "Those people actually get up and say, 'I know that Joseph Smith was a prophet of God.' That's just silly." I said, "Do you think so?" He said, "Yes, that's ridiculous." I said, "Well, I'll tell you what you do. You get baptized, and the next fast meeting you go to you will be confirmed a member of the Church. Then if you have enough nerve, you will stand up on your feet, and you will say the silliest thing you have ever said in all your life."

A year and a half later I received a message from him. He said, "I've been thinking about what you said. Next Tuesday we are all coming into the temple." I opened my eyes. I hadn't heard that he had joined the Church. He said, "You know, six months after you were out here, my eighteen-year-old boy was ordained a priest. I got to thinking about it, and I went to him, and I said, 'My boy, you go to the bishop and get permission to baptize your dad.' That's the fastest running I have ever seen in my life. He got permission, and he baptized me. The next fast meeting I went to, I was confirmed a member of the Church. I mustered up enough courage to stand upon my feet, and I said the most ridiculous thing I have ever said in all my life. I said, 'I know that Joseph Smith was a prophet of God.' Now we are all coming in next Tuesday." It was the year of all that snow; the trains were blocked. He said, "We are all coming into the temple, and we want you to be there." Well, I was there. We went into that room, and he and his wife knelt at the altar with their hands joined, and they were sealed for time and all eternity. Then we went out and brought in all those youngsters, and they knelt around the altar, and their hands joined with their parents, and there was that eighteen-year-old boy that was responsible for the whole thing. They were all sealed for time and for all eternity. The father is in the bishopric now. Last year I met his son back in the Eastern states. He is preaching the gospel to his father's relatives in Pennsylvania. His father is an oil man. . . . He is well-to-do, yet he is standing up and saying that silly thing. He has turned into being one of the greatest braggers I ever saw in all my life.

Matthew Cowley Speaks, pp. 93-94.

Biographical Sketch

PRESIDENT JEDEDIAH M. GRANT

Jedediah M. Grant was born on February 21, 1816, at Windsor, New York, the son of Joshua Grant and Athalia Howard.

At age seventeen he was converted to the Church and was baptized March 21, 1833.

Elder Grant served many missions. His first was in 1835.

Elder Grant was ordained a seventy February 28, 1835, under the hands of Joseph Smith, Sidney Rigdon and Frederick G. Williams. He was set apart on December 2, 1845, as one of the first Seven Presidents of the Seventies at age twenty-nine.

Elder Grant was elected as the first mayor of Salt Lake City. He was elected to that office in 1851.

He was chosen speaker of the house of representatives of the Utah territory in 1852.

Elder Jedediah Morgan Grant was ordained an apostle by President Brigham Young on April 7, 1854. He was sustained as President Young's second counselor on the same day. He was thirty-eight years old.

President Jedediah M. Grant was a zealous servant of

God and perhaps over-extended himself physically. He died at the early age of forty on December 1, 1856, in Salt Lake City.

At the time of his death one of his sons, Heber Jeddy Grant, who was to become the President of the Church, was just nine days old.

President Brigham Young paid Jedediah Morgan Grant a great compliment at Elder Grant's funeral services.

In essence he said:

"Jedediah has been a member of this Church some twenty-five years but in that time he has given the Lord one hundred years of church service."

JEDEDIAH M. GRANT

"Who Stands at the Head of Our Church?"

Elder Grant was challenged by a very eminent Baptist preacher, named Baldwin, to a discussion. Brother Grant consented. The place chosen was the fine, large church of his proud and imperious antagonist. Mr. Baldwin was described to me, as a man, overbearing in his manner—a regular browbeater. When the time came for the discussion, the house was densely crowded. Umpires were chosen, and everything was ready to proceed, when Brother Grant arose and said: "Mr. Baldwin, I would like to ask you a question before we proceed any farther." "Certainly so," said Baldwin. "Who stands at the head of your church in south-west Virginia?" Mr. Baldwin very quickly and austerely replied, "I do, sir; I do." "All right," said Brother Grant; "I wished to know that I had a worthy foe." Mr. Baldwin looked a little confused for a moment, and then said: "Mr. Grant, I would like to ask you, who stands at the head of your church in south-west Virginia?" Brother Grant arose and with bowed head replied, "Jesus Christ, sir." The shock was electrical. This inspired answer completely disarmed the proud foe, and the humble servant of God again came off victor.

Andrew Jenson, *The Latter-day Saints Biographical Encyclopedia* (Andrew Jenson History Company, 1901), p. 58.

"You See the Paper Is Blank"

In the early part of President Grant's ministry [as a missionary], he gained quite a reputation as a ready speaker, frequently responding to invitations to preach from such subjects or texts as might be selected at the time of commencing his sermon, by those inviting him. In time it became a matter of wonder with many as to how and when he prepared his wonderful sermons. In reply to their queries he informed them that he never prepared his sermons as other ministers did. "Of course, I read and store my mind with a knowledge of gospel truths," said he, "but I never study up a sermon." Well, they did not believe he told the truth, for, as they thought, it was impossible for a man to preach such sermons without careful preparation. So, in order to prove it, a number of persons decided to put him to test, and asked him if he would preach at a certain time and place, and from a text selected by them. They proposed to give him the text on his arrival at the place of meeting, thus giving him no time to prepare. To gratify them he consented. The place selected was Jeffersonville, the seat of Tazewell county, at that time the home of the late John B. Floyd, who subsequently became secretary of war, and many other prominent men. The room chosen was in the court house. At the hour appointed the house was packed to its capacity. Mr. Floyd and a number of lawyers and ministers were present and occupied front seats. Elder Grant came in, walked to the stand and opened the meeting as usual. At the close of the second hymn, a clerk, appointed for the occasion, stepped forward and handed the paper (the text) to Elder Grant, who unfolded it and found it to be blank. Without any mark of surprise, he held the paper up before the audience, and said: "My friends, I am here today according to agreement, to preach from such a text as these gentlemen might select for me. I have it here in my hand. I don't wish you to become offended at me, for I am under promise to preach from the text selected; and if any one is to blame, you must blame those who selected it. I knew nothing of what text they would choose, but of all texts this is my favorite one. You see the paper is blank (at the same time holding it up to view). You sectarians down there believe that out of nothing God created all things, and now you wish me to create a sermon from nothing, for this paper is blank. Now, you sectarians believe in a God that has neither body, parts nor passions. Such a God I conceive to be a perfect blank, just as you find my text is. You believe in a church without Prophets, Apostles, Evangelists, etc. Such a church would be a perfect blank, as compared with the Church of Christ, and this agrees with my text. You have located your heaven beyond the bounds of time and space. It exists nowhere, and consequently your heaven is blank, like unto my text." Thus he went on until he had torn to pieces all the tenets of faith professed by his hearers, and then proclaimed the principles of the gospel in great power. He wound up by asking, "Have I stuck to the text and does that satisfy you?" As soon as he sat down, Mr. Floyd jumped up and said, "Mr. Grant, if you are not a lawyer, you ought to be one." Then turning to the people, he added: "Gentlemen, you have listened to a wonderful discourse, and with amazement. Now, take a look at Mr. Grant's clothes. Look at his coat: his elbows are almost out: and his knees are almost through his pants. Let us take up a collection." As he sat down another eminent lawyer . . . arose and said: "I am good for one sleeve in a coat and one leg in a pair of pants, for Mr. Grant." The presiding elder of the M. E. Church, South, was requested to pass the hat around, but he replied that he would not take up a collection for a 'Mormon' preacher. "Yes you will," said Mr. Floyd; "Pass it around," said Mr. Stras, and the cry was taken up and repeated by the audience, until, for the sake of peace, the minister had to yield. He accordingly marched around with a hat in his hand, receiving contributions, which resulted in a collection sufficient to purchase a fine suit of clothes, a horse, saddle and bridle for Brother Grant, and not one contributor a member of The Church of Jesus Christ of Latter-day

Saints, though some joined subsequently. And this from a sermon produced from a blank text.

Andrew Jenson, *The Latter-day Saints Biographical Encyclopedia*, p. 57.

JEDEDIAH M. GRANT

"Here Is Little Margaret"

As told by Heber C. Kimball

I went to see him [Jedediah M. Grant] one day last week, and he reached out his hand and shook hands with me; he could not speak, but he shook hands warmly with me. I felt for him, and wanted to raise him up, and to have him stay and help us whip the devils and bring to pass righteousness. Why? Because he was valiant, and I loved him. . . .

I laid my hands upon him and blessed him, and asked God to strengthen his lungs that he might be easier, and in two or three minutes he raised himself up and talked for about an hour as busily as he could, telling me what he had seen and what he understood, until I was afraid he would weary himself, when I arose and left him.

He said to me, "Brother Heber, I have been into the spirit world two nights in succession, and, of all the dreads that ever came across me, the worst was to have to again return to my body, though I had to do it." But O, says he, "the order and government that were there! When in the spirit world, I saw the order of righteous men and women; beheld them organized in their several grades, and there appeared to be no obstruction to my vision; I could see every man and woman in their grade and order. I looked to see whether there was any disorder there, but there was none; neither could I see any death nor any darkness, disorder or confusion." He said that the people he there saw were organized in family capacities; and when he looked at them he saw grade after grade, and all were organized and in perfect harmony. He would mention one item after another and say, "Why, it is just as brother Brigham says it is; it is just as he has told us many a time."

That is a testimony as to the truth of what brother Brigham teaches us, and I know it is true. . . .

He saw the righteous gathered together in the spirit world, and there were no wicked spirits among them. He saw his wife; she was the first person that came to him. He saw many that he knew, but did not have conversation with any except his wife Caroline. She came to him, and he said that she looked beautiful and had their little child, that died on the Plains, in her arms, and said, ". . . Here is little Margaret; you know that the wolves ate her up, but it did not hurt her; here she is all right."[1]

"To my astonishment," he said, "when I looked at families there was a deficiency in some, there was a lack, for I saw families that would not be permitted to come and dwell together, because they had not honored their calling here."

He asked his wife Caroline where Joseph and Hyrum and Father Smith and others were; she replied, "They have gone away ahead, to perform and transact business for us." The same as when brother Brigham and his brethren left Winter Quarters and came here to search out a home; they came to find a location for their brethren.

He also spoke of the buildings he saw there, remarking that the Lord gave Solomon wisdom and poured gold and silver into his hands that he might display his skill and ability, and said that the temple erected by Solomon was much inferior to the most ordinary buildings he saw in the spirit world.

In regard to gardens, says brother Grant, "I have seen good gardens on this earth, but I never saw any to compare with those that were there. I saw flowers of numerous kinds, and some with

---

[1]Margaret had died on the plains and wolves dug up her grave.

from fifty to a hundred different colored flowers growing upon one stalk." We have many kinds of flowers on the earth, and I suppose those very articles came from heaven, or they would not be here.

After mentioning the things that he had seen, he spoke of how much he disliked to return and resume his body, after having seen the beauty and glory of the spirit world, where the righteous spirits are gathered together.

Heber C. Kimball, "Remarks at the Funeral of President Jedediah M. Grant," in *Journal of Discourses*, vol. 4, pp. 135-38.

Biographical Sketch

ELDER ALONZO A. HINCKLEY

Elder Hinckley was born April 23, 1870, at Cove Fort, Utah, a son of Ira Nathaniel Hinckley and Angeline Noble, New Englanders who helped to pioneer Utah. His ancestry is traced back to the early settlers of the American continent, who came in 1635. His father was a prominent pioneer, and his mother was one of the first school teachers in Salt Lake City, having taught in the old First Ward. Among her pupils was the mother of Maud Adams, world-famed actress.

In 1867, Brigham Young called his father to Cove Creek to supervise the building of the fort there.

Elder Hinckley's early life was spent in Cove Fort, his father moving to Fillmore when appointed president of Millard Stake in 1877.

A graduate of Fillmore grammar school and Brigham Young University, Elder Hinckley taught school for a number of years in Deseret, Millard County. As a dairyman, he aided his father and carried on his stock-raising interests after his father's death.

In 1892 he married Rose May Robison and lived in Deseret one year before moving to Hinckley, where he made his home. He left home on July 14, 1897, to spend three years in Holland on a mission. He was then the father of three children with the near advent of another.

Elder Hinckley served two terms in the legislature, representing Millard County. When Charles R. Mabey was elected governor, he appointed him state commissioner of agriculture.

Elder Hinckley was chosen in 1902, at the age of 32 years, to succeed his father as president of the Millard Stake and presided over that stake until it was divided into the Millard and Deseret Stakes.

From his early youth Elder Hinckley had assumed positions of leadership.

Following his release from the Millard Stake presidency, Elder Hinckley made his home for a short time in Salt Lake City, laboring as a special worker in the Salt Lake Temple, until his appointment as president of the California Mission.

On October 3, 1934, he was called to fill a vacancy in the Council of the Twelve Apostles caused by the death of President Anthony W. Ivins, to whom he bore a very striking resemblance.

While a member of the Council of Twelve he visited many of the stakes of the Church. However, his continuing ill health in 1935 caused him to relinquish his active duties and he spent most of the winter and summer of 1935-36 on the Pacific Coast recuperating from a serious ailment.

Elder Hinckley died December 22, 1936, at Salt Lake City, Utah. He was sixty-four years old.

The Improvement Era, February 1937.

ALONZO A. HINCKLEY

"I Was Understanding Dutch"

When I first arrived in Holland to fill a mission in 1897, I was unable to learn the language. I wrote home to my father and asked him to call upon the Bishop of the Ward, the Patriarch of the Stake, and other men in whom he had confidence, and invite them to join him in praying to the Lord in my behalf that I might acquire the language and be able to deliver my message to the people.

I had never sought for a sign because I was fearful of them, but I did seek the Spirit of the Lord to help me touch the hearts of men. I not only prayed to the Lord to assist me to learn the Dutch language, but I also studied it as faithfully as I could. I succeeded in learning two or three sentences which enabled me to deliver my literature from door to door.

One day, when I was alone, visiting among the people at Rotterdam, it was my duty to go back to the homes in which I had left tracts and take up the literature. As I went to gather the booklets, some power, that I cannot understand, possessed me until I quaked and trembled. I stood and looked at the house at which I was to call and felt as if I could not go to the door. But I knew my duty and so, with fortitude and determination I went to the house, raised the knocker and dropped it. Almost instantly, the door opened and an irate woman stepped out and closed it behind her. She talked in a very loud, shrill voice, berating me most severely.

I did not realize for the moment, that I was understanding Dutch as clearly as though she had been speaking English. I felt no supernatural power, or influence, or feeling. I just knew every word she was saying. She spoke so loudly that a carpenter, who was working across the street, building a porch on a little store, heard her and, I suppose, thought I was abusing the woman, for he came over to where we stood and brought his son with him and, greatly to my alarm, he carried a broadax. The man took his position near me and listened to the woman, who continued her tirade against me in a shouting voice.

I did not grow angry because of the woman's abuse, but to the contrary, my soul was filled with a burning desire to speak her language and to testify of the divinity of the Gospel and of the Lord Jesus Christ. I thought if I could only explain to her the importance of my message and the good it would do her, she would not berate me as she does now.

In a few moments she ceased her abuse and I began speaking. And I spoke the Dutch language. I defended the Truth and bore testimony of the restoration of the Gospel.

I had forgotten the large man who stood near me with his ax, and, as I looked at the woman and delivered my message of truth, he put his arms across my shoulders and, looking the woman in the face, said, "The Mormon Church may have its black sheep, but this is a man of God."

Her bitterness now gone, the woman replied, "I know it."

After the conversation, I went back home, hardly touching the ground. It dawned upon me that the prayers I had offered —and perhaps as a result, in part, of the hard study I had made —and the prayers of those at home, had been answered in a moment, for I had spoken the Dutch language intelligently for the first time in my life.

In ecstasy, I rushed home to tell Brother Thatcher in the office, and to tell the president of the mission; but when I attempted to speak, to my great dismay, I was the same as before. I could not understand nor speak the language.

President Farrell asked me if I would go to meeting that night.

"Yes, President Farrell," I answered, "after a man has been blessed of the Lord as I have been, I will gladly go. But I beg of you not to call upon me to speak even if you call upon someone to interpret what I say."

"Very well," he agreed, "I promise you, Brother Hinckley, that if you go you will not be asked to speak."

I went to meeting, and everything progressed nicely, as I thought, until Brother DeBry, the Branch President, arose and, contrary to Brother Farrell's promise, announced, "We shall now hear from Elder Hinckley."

President Farrell stepped forward, greatly embarrassed, and, addressing me, asked, "Brother Hinckley, shall I interpret for you?"

I felt a power I can not describe. "Wait, President Farrell," I said as I stood upon my feet. And then I began to speak, not in my native tongue, but in the Dutch language. And, then and there, I delivered the first discourse in my life in the tongue of that mission. The following morning I was sent to preside over the Amsterdam District.

Bryant S. Hinckley, *The Faith of Our Pioneer Fathers* (Deseret Book Company, 1959), pp. 231-33.

ALONZO A. HINCKLEY

"Was This Not a Beautiful Dream?"

While Elder Hinckley was on this mission to the Netherlands his second son was born. His heart was filled with great anxiety concerning the birth of this boy. When he received word from his wife that all was well, he wrote as follows:

"November 18, 1897. I have never received better news than I have received from you this morning. I am so happy and relieved of anxiety that I actually am beside myself. I cannot keep from laughing when I meet any one, and tell them of my good fortune. I am the most thankful man in Holland; and I tell you, it did not take me long to get on my knees and pour out my heart in gratitude to God for his mercies unto us.

"I have had such a lovely dream. I have been with you all—seen you, my dear wife, and the little newcomer, and all those kind ones who have surrounded you. I saw you made comfortable and happy. It seemed that I was in a hurry to get off again for Holland. But I first thanked all, with my heart so full of love that I gathered you all in my arms and embraced you, and then took one more peek in the door at Rose [his wife] and the children, and then landed back in Holland. Was this not a beautiful dream for one in my mood?"

In that far-off land he knew the very day and hour that his son was born and his heart was filled to overflowing with joy.

Hinckley, *The Faith of Our Pioneer Fathers*, p. 234.

ALONZO A. HINCKLEY

"I Am Prepared"

With 64 years of life behind him, and a record of dedicated service to the Lord, Alonzo Hinckley was called to serve as a member of the Council of the Twelve Apostles of The Church of Jesus Christ of Latter-day Saints.

Only a year later, he became seriously ill, and though he told few others, knew that the illness would be fatal. Thereupon, he wrote to the First Presidency of the Church, expressing a feeling of resignation and reiterating his testimony to the restoration of the Gospel.

The letter included these thoughts, manifesting the rich and abiding faith Elder Hinckley had in his Heavenly Father and his willingness to yield to His divine will:

I assure you, I am not deeply disturbed over the final results. I am reconciled and I reach my hands to take what my Father has for me, be it life or death. With a spirit of thanksgiving, and I trust free from vanity or boastfulness, I look over the past with satisfaction. I would not turn the leaf down on any chapter of my life. So far as I know, I have honored my Heavenly Father with my time, my humble talents and all the means that he has blessed me with and I have dealt justly with all men. I have fought, but I have fought fairly.

As to the future, I have no misgivings. It is inviting and glorious and I sense rather clearly what it means to be saved by the redeeming blood of Jesus Christ and to be exalted by his power and be with Him forever more.

My only concern is for the present. Life is and ever has been sweet indeed to me. My wife, my eternal companion, has been and is all in all to me. What a mother! What a wife! For her I grieve. The children are all right. Twelve of them are living: all are grown; all are pure, clean, wholesome, faithful fixed in their purpose, and devoted to the Church.

I come to one expression of regret—the possibly shortened period of intimate contact with you and the members of the Council of the Twelve. How I have longed to stand with you and thrust in my sickle with my might and reap a harvest for the Lord and then pass on when you could say, "He wrought valiantly to the end." If it is cut short now it will be hard for me to avoid thinking, "What an unprofitable servant."

I discovered my letter has reached undue proportions. It also seems to be gloomy. Quite to the contrary, I am not blue or despondant; I am prepared.[1]

---

[1]*Improvement Era*, February 1937, p. 77.

Biographical Sketch

Anthony W. Ivins was born on September 16, 1852, at Toms River, New Jersey, the son of Israel Ivins and Anna Lowrie.

He crossed the plains with his parents in 1853 when he was less than one year old. When he was nine years old, his parents were called by President Brigham Young to help "Utah's Dixie," and the city of St. George was established.

In 1881 he was chosen a member of the high council of St. George Stake, being ordained a high priest, and in 1882 was assigned missionary work in Mexico. He remained at Mexico City until 1884, being president of the Mexican Mission one year. In 1888 he was chosen first counselor to President Daniel D. McArthur of the St. George Stake, and remained in that post until 1895, when he was called by President Wilford Woodruff to go to Mexico and again take charge of church interests in that country. In 1896 he moved his family to Mexico, being appointed president of the Juarez Stake of Zion. He was also vice president and general manager of the Mexican Colonization and Agricultural Company and president of the Dublan Mercantile Company. He returned from Mexico in 1898.

Elder Ivins was chosen and sustained as a member of the Council of Twelve Apostles in October 1907, and was ordained October 6 by President Joseph F. Smith.

Anthony W. Ivins was sustained as second counselor to President Heber J. Grant March 10, 1921. He became first counselor to President Grant on May 28, 1925.

President Grant paid Anthony W. Ivins the following tribute: "His life has been devoted to the highest ideals. In everything he has striven to do his best. In many things he has excelled. In civil affairs he has served the people in many capacities, always with distinction and integrity. Not only is he a man of high moral courage, but he has proved himself on more than one occasion as a man of great physical courage, and when serving as deputy sheriff he exhibited the fearlessness of his nature by arresting some of the most desperate characters in the country. He served several terms as a member of the Territorial Legislature, where he was regarded as one of the outstanding leaders. He was also one of the framers of the State Constitution.

President Anthony Woodward Ivins died September 23, 1934, at Salt Lake City, Utah.

Jenson, *The L.D.S. Biographical Encyclopedia*, pp. 48-49.

ANTHONY W. IVINS

"His Mother Said Nothing But Tears Filled Her Eyes"

In the fall of 1861, the writer passed his ninth birthday. He resided, at the time, with his parents, in the Fifteenth Ward, Salt Lake City. . . .

One afternoon in October, 1861, the writer was at the home of John M. Moody, playing with other children, when a messenger came with the announcement that the Moody family had been called by the presiding authorities of the Church, to go to Dixie to raise cotton and develop the resources of that part of the territory. Frightened by the thought of such a move, he ran through the block to the home of his parents, and bursting into the house exclaimed to his mother and sister, who were in the room,

"Brother Moody is called to go to Dixie."

"So are we," said his sister, between sobs.

His mother said nothing, but tears filled her eyes as she thought of leaving a good home and comfortable surroundings, and of facing the hardships and dangers of frontier life, in the barren country known as Utah's Dixie.

Several hundred families had been so called to go upon this mission. It was the manner in which the affairs of the Church were conducted, at that time. . . .

Some offered excuses. Some were too poor to go, some were too rich . . . but the great majority, with that devotion which has characterized the members of the Church from the beginning, silently but resolutely made preparations for the accomplishment of the task assigned them.

Valuable homes were disposed of for but a small part of their real value. Farms were exchanged for teams or livestock which could be driven through to their destination; and the late fall and early winter of 1861 found hundreds of teams on the rough and dreary road to the South.

Nibley, *Pioneer Stories*, pp. 129-31.

ANTHONY W. IVINS

"Under Those High Cliffs"

When I was a boy, I had close friends, as all boys have, . . . among them was a boy about my own age. We lived near together; we went to school together. This boy had two older brothers. His parents were devoted Latter-day Saints. The country at that time was wild and lawless among the frontier. These older brothers became freighters; they loved horses and mules, and they delighted in putting together splendid teams, and drove those teams into Montana, and west into Nevada, and down to the coast in California, freighting back merchandise which in those days was needed for the use of the people. They became two of the most profane men I ever knew, indifferent to the faith of their fathers, and intemperate.

One day the body of the elder of those two boys was

brought into our town and his funeral services were held there. He had been killed in a difficulty with another man. The other, the next older brother, drifted away, and I lost sight of him. But this boy, who was my chum I grew up with, and pretty soon he obtained a team and he went off to Silver Reef to freight, and learned to swear, and he was following the very road that his older brothers had followed.

About that time I lost track of him. I went to Mexico. I came back after fifteen or twenty years, and had occasion to go up into Idaho to visit one of the stakes of the Church. I found this man there, presiding as bishop of one of the wards! I found one of his sons the bishop of another ward. I found another son president of the Mutual Improvement Association; and one or two of the boys had been on missions. He had a splendid home there, presided over in dignity by his good wife.

I looked at it all with wonder, and he smiled and said, "I know what you are thinking about."

I said, "Tell me how it all happened."

"Well," he said, "you know that I was going just the way my brothers went."

"Yes," I said. "That is what surprises me."

"My parents had always taught me a better way," he said. "They had urged me to read the scriptures, and finally I decided that I would read the Book of Mormon, and I did so while I was freighting. I read it through, and when I came to certain words in the last chapter of Moroni, I was very deeply impressed with them." These are the words to which he referred:

And I seal up these records, after I have spoken a few words by way of exhortation unto you.

Behold, I would exhort you that when ye shall read these things, if it be wisdom in God that ye should read them, that ye would remember how merciful the Lord hath been unto the children of men, from the creation of Adam, even down until the time that ye shall receive these things, and ponder it in your hearts.

And when ye shall receive these things, I would exhort you that ye would ask God, the Eternal Father, in the name of Christ, if these things are not true; and if ye shall ask with a sincere heart, with real intent, having faith in Christ, he will manifest the truth of it unto you, by the power of the Holy Ghost. (Moroni 10:2-4.)

101

He said, "When I read these words, I thought I would put the Lord to the test, and I stopped my team, wrapped the lines around the brake, and got down from that high seat, on one of those old-fashioned California wagons that were common in early days, and I turned off from the road; and you remember that piece of straight road," he said, "just below the twist?"

"Yes," I said, "I remember every rock there is on it, because I have freighted over it."

"Well, I went out there," he said, "under those high cliffs to the east of the road, and went around behind some rocks where no one could see me, kneeled down there, and thought I would pray, and I couldn't say a word.

"But," he said, "by making a great effort I managed to appeal to the Lord, told him that I wanted to know the truth, and I want to tell you that those fellows on the day of Pentecost never received a stronger testimony than I did; I felt that I was surrounded by consuming fire, and I got up on my feet knowing just as well that the Lord lived, that Christ was the Redeemer of the World, that the gospel had been restored through the Prophet Joseph Smith, and that the Book of Mormon is a divine record, as I knew that I was there; and I got on my wagon, drove home, left the road and came up here, located on this quarter section of land, and you can see the rest."

Hinckley, *The Faith of Our Pioneer Fathers,* pp. 187-90.

"The Indians Left Them"

During the year of 1865 the Navajo Indians were at war with the Government. Hard pressed in their own country, the Northeastern part of Arizona and Northwestern New Mexico, small parties of Indians came across the Colorado River and made raids upon the white settlers who had located in the extreme southeastern part of Utah. . . .

Because of these and other depredations, the people were called in from outlying settlements and exposed ranches, to places of safety.

Nathan C. Tenney had established a ranch at Short Creek where he built a house, but in common with others had abandoned it, and moved to Toquerville, about twenty-five miles distant.

In December, 1866, three horsemen rode out from Toquerville, their destination being the Short Creek Ranch. They were fairly well mounted, and in those early days would have been considered well armed. Nathan C. Tenney carried an old-fashioned cap-and-ball pistol. Enoch Dodge was armed with a light, muzzle-loading rifle. The third member of the party, Ammon M. Tenney, was a mere boy, with black hair, dark eyes and a slender body. He carried an old style six-shooter, and was going with his father to look for horses which had strayed from Toquerville back to the ranch.

The party reached Short Creek without incident, and spent the night at the ranch house. The following morning they rode out on the Pipe Spring trail to the place where the Berry Brothers had been killed, and after looking over the ground, went on and soon found the horses for which they were hunting.

Not far from them was one of those peculiar hills, or ridges, so common on the Short Creek range. By some convulsion of nature these ridges have been forced up, leaving an abrupt face of rock, often impossible of ascent, on the east or north, while on the west or south they gradually dip to the plains below so that approach to the top of the cliffs from that side is easy.

At the foot of one of these bluffs, a corral had been constructed to which the horses, eight in number, were driven and hurriedly caught and necked together. Signs indicating to the trained eyes of these experienced frontiersmen that Indians were in the neighbrohood had been observed and commented upon, and that feeling of anxiety which comes to men who sense impending danger that cannot be seen was intense.

The horses were driven from the corral and headed toward home, when the white men found themselves face to face with eight Navajos. The Indians, spread out in a semi-circle, occupied the plain, while the white men retired to the protection of the cliffs to which reference has been made. What was to be done? That the Indians meant to kill them was plain to the two men. Their weapons, consisting of bows and arrows and a few guns, were made ready as they taunted and denounced the white men.

To Nathan C. Tenney, a man who had many times looked death in the face, the situation appeared desperate, hopeless. With the impassable cliffs behind, and Indians in front, what chance had they to escape? The boy proposed that all of the horses be killed and used as a breastwork, and that they fight. The father urged that their ammunition would soon be exhausted and they slaughtered. They thought it possible to compromise by giving up their horses.

The boy spoke to the Indians in Spanish, which language he had learned in California, and found that he was understood. A parley ensued, and one of the Indians, a stalwart man, leaving his arms, came out into the circle and invited the boy to meet him there and arrange terms of capitulation. Removing his pistol, the boy was about ready to comply when his father restrained him. "My son," he said, "that powerful man, will pick you up and carry you away, and then they will kill us."

At this juncture the cliffs echoed with war whoops, and to their dismay the men saw eight additional Indians riding furiously down the plain toward them, their long hair streaming behind as they unslung their guns and quivers.

"Resistance is now useless," said the elder Tenney. "What hope have we against sixteen well armed and mounted men?" It was at this juncture that the courage and leadership of the boy asserted itself. Drawing his pistol, he turned down the trail at the base of the bluff, and striking the spurs deep into his horse's sides, and crying "Follow me!", rode straight on the Indians, who confronted him, firing as he went. The two men followed. Against this intrepid charge, the Indians gave way, and the race for life began. Thus, for more than a mile they rode, the three on the trail, sheltered to the west by the bluff, while the Indians, who were in front of them, behind them, and on the plain to the east, kept up a constant fusilade of shots as they ran.

Several times the boy, who was a superb horseman, and better mounted, had opportunity to outstrip his pursuers and escape, and often he returned to encourage his father and Dodge to be brave and come on. He was thus riding in advance when a sharp cry from his father caused him to look back to see both horse and rider rolling in the dust. The Indians, with bows bent to the arrowheads, were bearing down on his father in a body. Without a moment's hesitation the boy turned and spurred his horse between his father and the on-rushing savages, discharging his pistol in the very faces of the men nearest him. The Indians wavered, scattered, and, falling on the opposite side of their horses, discharged a volley at the boy.

His father declared that he had been shot; and Dodge, also having been wounded, they implored the boy to escape and go to his mother. Instead of doing this, he assisted his father to his feet, and turning the horses loose, with the saddles on, urged the men to climb to the rocks above. For a few moments the attention of the Indians was attracted to the loose horses and during this time the boy succeeded in getting the men up into the rocks, where he covered their retreat, while the Indians, riding by at the foot of the bluff, in single file, kept up a constant fire on him.

When the upper ledge was reached, the situation again

looked hopeless; the cliff presented an obstacle which the men declared it would be impossible to pass, but the boy, undismayed, made the effort and succeeded. He then took hold of the gun, and while his father held on, he pulled, and Dodge pushed until the father reached the top where he fell unconscious. With the gun, he then pulled Dodge to the summit.

A hasty examination showed that the father had not been shot, as he thought, but that the fall from the horse had dislocated and badly bruised his shoulder. Dodge had been shot in the leg. The boy lay down on his back, took his father's hand in his, and placing one foot on the neck, the other in the arm pit, with a quick jerk and strong twist, brought the dislocated joint back into place. He then placed his hands upon the head of his father, and in a few well-chosen words, laid their condition before the Lord, and prayed that his father might be restored. The man arose and they retreated a short distance to the west where they concealed themselves in some loose rocks. They had scarcely done so when they heard the patter of the feet of the Indians, on the very rocks under which they had taken refuge.

Darkness came on and with it the Indians left them, thinking, undoubtedly, that they had made good their escape and were far away. When it appeared safe, they came out from their hiding place, and guided by the boy, slowly made their way to Duncan's Retreat, from which they were taken to their home by friends.

Nibley, *Pioneer Stories*, pp. 138-44.

Biographical Sketch

Elder Kimball was born June 16, 1801, at Shelden, Vermont, to Solomon Kimball and Anna Spaulding.

In the fall of 1831 Elder Kimball first met Mormon missionaries. In April 1832 he was baptized.

He was called to be an apostle in 1835 and was a member of the first Quorum of Twelve in this dispensation.

He served as a missionary to Canada and New England in 1835. In 1837 he was called to open the missionary work in England. During this mission of less than a year he was responsible for 1,500 baptisms.

Elder Kimball returned to England with other members of the Twelve in 1840.

He was one of the first pioneers to come into the Salt Lake Valley in 1847.

Elder Kimball was sustained as first counselor to President Brigham Young in 1847, a position he held until his death on June 22, 1868, at age sixty-seven.

Heber Chase Kimball lived an exemplary life; he had a great gift of prophecy and was deeply loved by the Latter-day Saints.

Few men in the history of the Church have been loved and honored as was Heber C. Kimball. He was fearless, and no one could doubt his integrity and his complete devotion to the Lord Jesus Christ.

HEBER C. KIMBALL

"The Faith of a Little Child"

During the winter of 1834-1835 a theological school was established in Kirtland. It was the custom at the school to call upon a certain member to speak for the edification of the others. Heber C. Kimball, on one occasion, was invited to address them on the subject of faith. He began by relating an incident that had occurred but recently in his own family. "My wife, one day," commenced Brother Kimball, "when going out on a visit, gave our daughter Helen Mar charge not to touch the dishes," as they were very scarce, expensive, and hard to replace. She advised her that if she broke any during her absence, she would punish her when she returned. "While my wife was absent," continued Brother Kimball, "My daughter broke a number of the dishes by letting the table leaf fall. . . ."

The little girl was greatly frightened and "went out under an apple tree and prayed that her mother's heart might be softened, that when she returned she would not spank her. "Her mother was very punctual," said Brother Kimball, "when she made a promise to her children, to fulfill it, and when she returned, she undertook, as a duty, to carry this promise into effect. She retired with [the little girl] into her room, but found herself powerless to chastise her; her heart was so softened that it was impossible for her to raise her hand against the child. Afterwards, Helen told her mother she had prayed to the Lord that she might not whip her."

Brother Heber paused in his simple narrative. Tears glistened in the eyes of his listeners; the Prophet Joseph who was a warm and tender-hearted man, was also weeping. He told the brethren that that was the kind of faith they needed: "the faith of a little child, going in humility to its parents, and asking for the desire of its heart." He complimented Brother Kimball and said "the anecdote was well-timed."

Conference Report, October 1970, p. 20.

HEBER C. KIMBALL

"I Slipped Through the Door and Escaped"

"**W**e were very much grieved," says Heber, "on our arrival in Kirtland, to see the spirit of speculation that was prevailing in the Church. . . .

"The Prophet Joseph says of those times: 'The spirit of speculation in lands and property of all kinds, which was so prevalent throughout the whole nation, was taking deep root in the Church. As the fruits of this spirit, evil surmising, fault-finding, disunion, dissension and apostasy followed in quick succession, and it seemed as though all the powers of earth and hell were combining their influence in an especial manner to overthrow the Church at once and make a final end. The enemy abroad and apostates in our midst united in their schemes. . . .'

"This order of things," continues Heber, "increased during the winter to such an extent that a man's life was in danger the moment he spoke in defence of the Prophet of God. During this time I had many days of sorrow and mourning, for my heart sickened to see the awful extent that things were getting to. The only source of consolation I had, was in bending my knees continually before my Father in Heaven, and asking Him to sustain me and preserve me from falling into snares, and from betraying my brethren as others had done; for those who apostatized sought every means and opportunity to draw others after them. They also entered into combinations to obtain wealth by fraud and every means that was evil.

"At this time, I had many dreams from the Lord; one of them I will relate. I dreamed that I entered the house of John F. Boynton, in which there was a panther; he was jet black and very beautiful to look upon, but he inspired me with fear; when I rose to leave the house he stood at the door with the intention to seize on me, and seeing my fear, he displayed his beauty to me, telling me how sleek his coat was and what beautiful ears he had, and also his claws, which appeared to be of silver, and then he showed me his teeth, which also appeared to be silver. John F. Boynton told me that if I made myself familiar with him he would not hurt me, but if I did not he would. I did not feel disposed to do so and while the panther was displaying to me his beauty, I slipped through the door and escaped although he tried to keep me back by laying hold of my coat; but I rent myself from him. The interpretation of this dream was literally fulfilled. The panther represented an apostate whom I had been very familiar with. I felt to thank the Lord for this dream and other intimations that I had, which, by His assistance kept me from falling into snares."

Orson F. Whitney, *Life of Heber C. Kimball* (Bookcraft, 1967), pp. 99-102.

"Big Tears Rolled Down His Cheeks"

On Sunday, the 4th day of June, 1837, [says Heber C. Kimball,] the Prophet Joseph came to me, while I was seated in front of the stand, above the sacrament table, on the Melchizedek side of the Temple, in Kirtland, and whispering to me, said, "Brother Heber, the Spirit of the Lord has whispered to me: 'Let my servant Heber go to England and proclaim my Gospel, and open the door of salvation to that nation. . . .' "

Feeling my weakness to go upon such an errand, I asked the Prophet if Brother Brigham might go with me. He replied that he wanted Brother Brigham to stay with him, for he had something else for him to do. The idea of such a mission was almost more than I could bear up under. I was almost ready to sink under the burden which was placed upon me.

However, all these considerations did not deter me from the path of duty; the moment I understood the will of my heavenly Father, I felt a determination to go at all hazards, believing that He would support me by His almighty power, and endow me with every qualification that I needed; and although my family was dear to me, and I should have to leave them almost destitute, I felt that the cause of truth, the Gospel of Christ, outweighed every other consideration. . . .

The Presidency laid their hands on me and set me apart to preside over the mission, and conferred great blessings upon my head; said that God would make me mighty in that nation in winning souls unto Him; angels should accompany me and bear me up, that my feet should never slip; that I should be mightily blessed and prove a source of salvation to thousands, not only in England but America.

After being called on this mission, I daily went into the east room in the attic story of the temple and poured out my soul unto the Lord, asking His protection and power to fulfill honorably the mission appointed me by His servants. . . .

[The day of departure came; Tuesday, June 13th, 1837. The solemn scene of Heber's parting with his family cannot be more tenderly or graphically told than in the words of Elder Robert B. Thompson, who thus describes it:]

The day appointed for the departure of the Elders to England having arrived, I stepped into the house of Brother Kimball to ascertain when he would start, as I expected to accompany him two or three hundred miles, intending to spend my labors in Canada that season.

The door being partly open, I entered and felt struck with the sight which presented itself to my view. I would have retired, thinking that I was intruding, but I felt riveted to the spot. The father was pouring out his soul to that "God who rules on high," that he would grant him a prosperous voyage across the mighty ocean, and make him useful wherever his lot should be cast, and that He who "careth for sparrows, and feedeth the young ravens when they cry" would supply the wants of his wife and little ones in his absence. He then, like the patriarchs, and by virtue of his office, laid his hands upon their heads individually, leaving a father's blessing upon them, and commending them to the care and protection of God, while he should be engaged preaching the Gospel in a foreign land. While thus engaged his voice almost lost in the sobs of those around, who tried in vain to suppress them. The idea of being separated from their protector and father for so long a time was indeed painful. He proceeded, but his heart was too much affected to do so regularly. His emotions were great, and he was obliged to stop at intervals, while the big tears rolled down his cheeks, an index to the feelings which reigned in his bosom. My heart was not stout enough to refrain; in spite of myself I wept, and mingled my tears with theirs. At the same time I felt thankful that I had the privilege of contemplating such a scene. I realized that nothing could induce that man to tear himself from so affectionate a family group, from his partner and children who were so dear to

him—nothing but a sense of duty and love to God and attach-
ment to His cause.

Whitney, *Life of Heber C. Kimball* (Bookcraft), pp. 103-109.

———

HEBER C. KIMBALL

"A Scene of Satanic Power"

"Saturday evening," says Heber
C. Kimball, "it was agreed that I should go forward and bap-
tize, the next morning, in the river Ribble, which runs through
Preston [England].

"By this time the adversary of souls began to rage, and he
felt determined to destroy us before we had fully established the
kingdom of God in that land, and the next morning I witnessed a
scene of satanic power and influence which I shall never forget.

"Sunday, July 30th, about daybreak, Elder Isaac Russell
(who had been appointed to preach on the obelisk in Preston
Square, that day,) who slept with Elder Richards in Wilfred
Street, came up to the third story, where Elder Hyde and myself were sleeping, and called out, 'Brother Kimball, I want you
should get up and pray for me that I may be delivered from the
evil spirits that are tormenting me to such a degree that I feel
I cannot live long, unless I obtain relief.'

"I had been sleeping on the back of the bed. I immediately
arose, slipped off at the foot of the bed, and passed round to
where he was. Elder Hyde threw his feet out, and sat up in
the bed, and we laid hands on him, I being mouth, and prayed
that the Lord would have mercy on him, and rebuked the
devil.

116

"While thus engaged, I was struck with great force by some invisible power, and fell senseless on the floor. The first thing I recollected was being supported by Elders Hyde and Richards, who were praying for me; Elder Richards having followed Russell up to my room. Elders Hyde and Richards then assisted me to get on the bed, by my agony was so great I could not endure it, and I arose, bowed my knees and prayed. I then arose and sat up on the bed, when a vision was opened to our minds, and we could distinctly see the evil spirits, who foamed and gnashed their teeth at us. We gazed upon them about an hour and a half (by Willard's watch). We were not looking towards the window, but towards the wall. Space appeared before us, and we saw the devils coming in legions, with their leaders, who came within a few feet of us. They came towards us like armies rushing to battle. They appeared to be men of full stature, possessing every form and feature of men in the flesh, who were angry and desperate; and I shall never forget the vindictive malignity depicted on their countenances as they looked me in the eye; and any attempt to paint the scene which then presented itself, or portray their malice and enmity, would be vain. I perspired exceedingly, my clothes becoming as wet as if I had been taken out of the river. I felt excessive pain, and was in the greatest distress for some time. I cannot even look back on the scene without feelings of horror; yet by it I learned the power of the adversary, his enmity against the servants of God, and got some understanding of the invisible world. We distinctly heard those spirits talk and express their wrath and hellish designs against us. However, the Lord delivered us from them, and blessed us exceedingly that day."

Elder Hyde's supplemental description of that fearful scene is as follows, taken from a letter addressed to President Kimball:

"Every circumstance that occurred at that scene of devils is just as fresh in my recollection at this moment as it was at the moment of its occurrence, and will ever remain so. After you were overcome by them and had fallen, their awful rush upon me with knives, threats, imprecations and hellish grins, amply convinced me that they were no friends of mine. While you were apparently senseless and lifeless on the floor and upon the bed (after we had laid you there), I stood between you and the devils and fought them and contended with them face to face, until they began to diminish in number and to retreat from the room. . . ."

Years later, narrating the experience of that awful morning to the Prophet Joseph, Heber asked him what it all meant, and whether there was anything wrong with him that he should have such a manifestation.

"No, Brother Heber," he replied, "at that time you were nigh unto the Lord; there was only a veil between you and Him, but you could not see Him. When I heard of it, it gave me great joy, for I then knew that the work of God had taken root in that land. It was this that caused the devil to make a struggle to kill you."

Joseph then related some of his own experience, in many contests he had had with the evil one, and said: "The nearer a person approaches the Lord, a greater power will be manifested by the adversary to prevent the accomplishment of His purposes."

Referring to the morning of his contest with the demons, Apostle Kimball says:

"Notwithstanding the weakness of my body from the shock I had experienced, I had the pleasure, about 9 a.m. of baptizing nine individuals and hailing them brethren and sisters in the kingdom of God. These were the first persons baptized into the Church in a foreign land, and only the eighth day after our arrival in Preston.

"A circumstance took place which I cannot refrain from mentioning, for it will show the eagerness and anxiety of some in that land to obey the Gospel. Two of the male candidates, when they had changed their clothes at a distance of several rods from the place where I was standing in the water, were so anxious to obey the Gospel that they ran with all their might to the water, each wishing to be baptized first. The younger, George D. Watt, being quicker of foot than the elder, outran him, and came first into the water.

"The circumstance of baptizing in the open air being somewhat novel, a concourse of between seven and nine thousand persons assembled on the banks of the river to witness the ceremony. . . ."

Whitney, *Life of Heber C. Kimball* (Bookcraft), pp. 129-32, 135.

HEBER C. KIMBALL

"Please, Sir, Will You Baptize Me?"

My sheep know my voice, and a stranger they will not follow."

A remarkable instance of this truth now occurred in Heber's ministry. Says he:

Having mentioned my intention of going to Downham and Chatburn, to several of the brethren, they endeavoured to dissuade me from going, informing me there could be no prospect of success whatever, as several ministers of different denominations had endeavored in vain to raise churches in these places, and had frequently preached to them, but to no effect, as they had resisted all the efforts and withstood the attempts of all sects and parties for the last thirty years, who, seeing all their attempts fail, had given them up to hardness of heart. I was also informed they were very wicked places. However, this did not discourage me, believing that the Gospel of Jesus Christ could reach the heart, when the gospels of men proved abortive; I consequently told those brethren that these were the places I wanted to go to, for that it was my business not to call the righteous but sinners to repentance.

The next day we received a very pressing invitation to

preach in Chatburn, but having given out an appointment to preach in Clithero that evening, I informed them that I would not be able to comply with their request that night; this did not satisfy them, they continued to solicit me with the greatest importunity, until I was obliged to consent to remain with them, and requested Elder Fielding to attend to the appointment at Clithero. . . .

In Chatburn I was cordially received by the inhabitants, who turned out in great numbers to hear me preach. They procured a large tithing barn, placing a barrel in the center, upon which I stood. I preached to them the first principles of the Gospel, spoke in simplicity upon the principles revealed by our Lord and Savior Jesus Christ, the conditions of pardon for a fallen world and the blessings and privileges of those who embraced the truth; I likewise said a little on the subject of the resurrection. My testimony was accompanied by the Spirit of the Lord, and was received with joy, and these people who had been represented as being hard and obdurate, were melted into tenderness and love. I told them that, being a servant of the Lord Jesus Christ, I stood ready at all times to administer the ordinances of the Gospel, and explained what was necessary to prepare them for baptism; that when they felt to repent of and forsake their sins, they were ready to be baptized for the remission of sins, like the jailor and his household, and Cornelius and his house. When I concluded I felt someone pulling at my coat. . . . I turned round and asked what was wanted. Mrs. Elizabeth Partington said, "Please sir, will you baptize me?" "And me?" "And me?" exclaimed more than a dozen voices. Accordingly I went down into the water and baptized twenty-five. I was engaged in this duty, and confirming them and conversing with the people until after midnight.

The next morning I returned to Downham, and baptized between twenty-five and thirty in the course of the day.

The next evening I returned to Chatburn. The congregation was so numerous that I had to preach in the open air, and took my stand on a stone wall, and afterwards baptized several. These villages seemed to be affected from one end to the other; parents called their children together, spoke to them on the subjects which I had preached about, and warned them against swearing and all other evil practices, and instructed them in their duty.

We were absent from Preston five days, during which time Brother Fielding and I baptized and confirmed about 110 persons; organized branches in Downham, Chatburn, Waddington and Clithero; and ordained several to the lesser Priesthood, to preside. This was the first time the people in those villages ever heard our voices, or saw an American.

I cannot refrain from relating an occurrence which took place while Brother Fielding and myself were passing through the village of Chatburn on our way to Downham: having been observed approaching the village, the news ran from house to house, and immediately the noise of their looms was hushed, and the people flocked to their doors to welcome us and see us pass. More than forty young people of the place ran to meet us; some took hold of our mantles and then of each others' hands; several having hold of hands went before us singing the songs of Zion, while their parents gazed upon the scene with delight, and poured their blessings upon our heads, and praised the God of heaven for sending us to unfold the principles of truth and the plan of salvation to them. The children continued with us to Downham, a mile distant. Such a scene, and such gratitude, I never witnessed before. "Surely," my heart exclaimed, "out of the mouths of babes and sucklings thou hast perfected praise." What could have been more pleasing and delightful than such a manifestation of gratitude to Almighty God; and from those whose hearts were deemed too hard to be penetrated by the Gospel, and who had been considered the most wicked and hardened people in that region of country."

Whitney, *Life of Heber C. Kimball* (Bookcraft), pp. 169-72.

"Willard, I Baptized Your Wife To-day"

On Wednesday, August 2nd," says Elder Kimball, "Miss Jennetta Richards, a young lady, the daughter of a minister of the Independent Order, who resided at Walkerfold, about fifteen miles from Preston, came to the house of Thomas Walmesley, with whom she was acquainted. Calling in to see them at the time she was there, I was introduced to her, and we immediately entered into conversation on the subject of the Gospel. I found her very intelligent. She seemed very desirous to hear the things I had to teach and to understand the doctrines of the gospel. I informed her of my appointment to preach that evening, and invited her to attend. She did so; and likewise the evening following. After attending these two services she was fully convinced of the truth.

"Friday morning, 4th, she sent for me, desiring to be baptized, which request I cheerfully complied with, in the river Ribble, and confirmed her at the water side, Elder Hyde assisting. . . . The following day she started for home, and wept as she was about to leave us. I said to her, 'Sister, be of good cheer, for the Lord will soften the heart of thy father, that I will yet have the privilege of preaching in his chapel, and it shall result in a great opening to preach the Gospel in that region.' I exhorted her to pray and be humble. She requested me to pray for her, and gave me some encouragement to expect that her father would open his chapel for me to preach in. I then hastened to my brethren, told them of the circumstances and the result of my visit with the young lady, and called upon them to unite with me in prayer that the Lord would soften the heart of her father, that he might be induced to open his chapel for us to preach in. . . ."

And now came the fulfillment of Heber's prophecy to

Jennetta Richards, daughter of the minister of Walkerfold. The early part of the week brought two letters to Elder Kimball, one from Miss Richards and the other from her father. The latter read as follows:

Mr. H. C. Kimball,

Sir:—You are expected to be here next Sunday. You are given out to preach in the forenoon, afternoon and evening. Although we be strangers to one another, yet, I hope we are not strangers to our blessed Redeemer, else I would not have given out for you to preach. Our chapel is but small and the congregation few,—yet if one soul be converted it is of more value than the whole world.

I remain, in haste,
JOHN RICHARDS.

While laboring in this neighborhood, Heber had a dream in which Willard Richards appeared to him and said: "You are wanted at Preston, and we cannot do without you any longer."

"The next morning," says he, "I started for Preston where I found that I was anxiously expected by the brethren. . . ."

Another of Heber's prophecies—one of those seemingly casual though fateful utterances for which he was famous—must here be mentioned.

"Willard, I baptized your wife to-day," were his words addressed to Elder Richards just after Jennetta Richards joined the Church. Willard and Jennetta had not yet seen each other. The sequel is in Willard's own words, taken from his diary. Time: March, 1838:

"I took a tour through the branches, and preached. While walking in Thornly I plucked a snowdrop, far through the hedge, and carried it to James Mercer's and hung it up in his kitchen. Soon after, Jennetta Richards came into the room, and I walked with her and Alice Parker to Ribchester, and attended meeting with Brothers Kimball and Hyde at Brother Clark's.

"While walking with these sisters, I remarked, 'Richards is a good name; I never want to change it; do you, Jennetta?' 'No; I do not,' was her reply, 'and I think I never will.'

"September 24th, 1839, I married Jennetta Richards, daughter of the Rev. John Richards, independent minister at Walkerfold, Chaigley, Lancashire. Most truly do I praise my Heavenly

123

Father for his great kindness in providing me a partner according to His promise. I receive her from the Lord, and hold her at His disposal. I pray that He may bless us forever. Amen!"

Whitney, *Life of Heber C. Kimball* (Bookcraft), pp. 137-44.

HEBER C. KIMBALL

"The Work of Eight Months"

It being known that the Elders were about to leave England, great numbers flocked to hear them, and many were baptized. Their labors were consequently very arduous. Says Elder Kimball:

"Some days we went from house to house, conversing with the people on the things of the kingdom, and would sometimes be instrumental in convincing many of the truth: and I have known as many as twenty persons baptized in one day, who have been convinced on such occasions. I have had to go into the water to administer the ordinance of baptism six or seven times a day, and frequently after having come out of the water and changed my clothes, I have had to turn back to the water before I reached my lodgings; this, too, when the weather was extremely cold, the ice being from twelve to fourteen inches thick. The weather continued so about twelve weeks, during which time I think there were but ten days in which we were not in the water baptizing. The harvest was indeed plenteous, but the laborers were few.

"Great numbers were initiated into the Kingdom of Heaven; those who were sick were healed; those who were diseased flocked to us daily; and truly their faith was great, such as I hardly ever witnessed before, consequently many were healed of their infirmities. We were continually employed day and night, and some nights hardly closing our eye-lids. The task was almost more than we could endure; but realizing the circumstances of this people, their love of the truth, their humility and unfeigned charity, caused us to use all diligence and make good use of every moment, for truly our bowels yearned over them."

Touching the prospects of the missionary work in England, he adds:

"The work kept spreading; the prospect of usefulness grew brighter and brighter, and the field opened larger and larger; while the cries of 'Come, and administer the words of life unto us,' were more and more frequently sounding in our ears. I do not remember during the last six months I was in England of retiring to my bed earlier than midnight, which was also the case with Brothers Hyde and Fielding.

"Sunday, April 8th, the day of the conference, came. The Saints began to assemble at an early hour. By nine o'clock there were from six to seven hundred present from various parts of the country. After the meeting was opened by singing and prayer . . . the total number of Saints represented was about two thousand. . . ."

All this was the work of only eight months. Two thousand had been baptized and enough branches organized to form the base work of three or four conferences, incorporating in the missionary work about that number of the counties of England. Thus the work had already widely spread, yet only three or four Elders had been out in the ministry. Heber C. Kimball himself had converted in eight months about one thousand five hundred souls.

Whitney, *Life of Heber C. Kimball* (Bookcraft), pp. 187-91.

"I Wept for Several Miles"

We left Apostles Kimball and Hyde, with their associates in the ministry, visiting the various branches of the mission they had founded, preparatory to taking farewell leave of the Saints and sailing for America. They agreed to hold a general conference in Preston on the 8th of April, the day before their departure. . . .

In the interval, writes Heber, "I went and visited the branches in the regions of Clithero and Chatburn, and on the morning when I left Chatburn many were in tears, thinking they should see my face no more. When I left them, my feelings were such as I cannot describe. As I walked down the street I was followed by numbers; the doors were crowded by the inmates of the houses to bid me farewell, who could only give vent to their grief in sobs and broken accents. While contemplating this scene I was constrained to take off my hat, for I felt as if the place was holy ground. The Spirit of the Lord rested down upon me and I was constrained to bless that whole region of country. I was followed by a great number to Clithero, a considerable distance from the villages, who could then hardly separate from me. My heart was like unto theirs, and I thought my head was a fountain of tears, for I wept for several miles after I bid them adieu. I had to leave the road three times to go to streams of water to bathe my eyes."

"Who can read this," says Tullidge, beautifully, "without feeling of profound veneration for the great and good man whose memory is enshrined in the hearts of the British Saints as their spiritual father? That touching scene is enough to immortalize the character of Heber C. Kimball as a true apostle of Christ; and the pathos is actually heightened when he is seen alone by the wayside weeping, or by the streams washing away those sacred tears."

Heber C. Kimball was indeed a true apostle of Christ, one

of the called and chosen; a prophet and a servant of God, in nature as well as name.

The Prophet Joseph told him in after years that the reason he felt as he did in the streets of Chatburn was because the place was indeed "holy ground," that some of the ancient prophets had traveled in that region and dedicated the land, and that he, Heber, had reaped the benefit of their blessing. . . .

". . . When we spoke of our departure their souls were melted; they gave vent to their feelings and wept like little children, and broke out in lamentations like the following: 'How can we part with our beloved brethren!' 'We may never see them again!' 'O, why must you leave us!' I could not restrain my feelings, and they found vent in a flood of tears. It would have been almost an impossibility for us to have left this affectionate people, if we had not had the most implicit confidence in the brethren who had been appointed to preside over them in our absence; but knowing they had the confidence of the Church, we felt that affairs would be conducted in righteousness. . . ."

At nine o'clock on the morning of April 9th, Elders Kimball, Hyde and Russell left Preston for Liverpool. Through the kindness of the Saints, many of whom assembled to bid them farewell, they were provided with means to take them back to Kirtland. With tearful eyes they were gazed at by the multitude until the coach was lost to view. . . .

"After a ride of about four hours we arrived at Liverpool." It was on the 20th of April, 1838, that the Elders embarked for home. ". . . Sunday, July 20th, I met Joseph, Sidney and Hyrum on the public square, as they started for Adam-On-di-Ahman. Joseph requested me to preach to the Saints and give them a history of my mission, saying, 'It will revive their spirits and do them good,' which I did, although I was scarcely able to stand. I related many things respecting my mission and travels, which were gladly received by them, whose hearts were cheered by the recital, while many of the Elders were stirred up to diligence, and expressed a great desire to accompany me when I should return to England."

Whitney, *Life of Heber C. Kimball* (Bookcraft), pp. 187-88, 194, 204.

"States Goods"

The year 1848 was the year of the cricket plague. Myriads of these destructive pests, an army of famine and despair, rolled in black legions down the mountain sides and attacked the growing fields of grain. The tender crops fell an easy prey to their fierce voracity. They literally swept everything before them. Starvation with all its terrors seemed staring the poor settlers in the face.

They were saved by a miracle. In the midst of the work of destruction, when it seemed as if nothing could stay the devastation, great flocks of gulls suddenly appeared. . . . They came to prey upon the destroyers. All day long they gorged themselves, and, when full, disgorged and feasted again. . . .

Still there was a season of scarcity. The surplus of the first harvests in the Valley had barely been sufficient to meet the wants of the emigration, which had commenced pouring in from the frontiers and from Europe; and now that the crickets had played such havoc with the crops, there was danger, in spite of the interposition of the gulls, of some suffering from hunger. . . .

It was during this time of famine, when the half starved, half-clad settlers scarcely knew where to look for the next crust of bread or for rags to hide their nakedness—for clothing had become almost as scarce with them as bread-stuffs—that Heber C. Kimball, filled with the spirit of prophecy, in a public meeting declared to the astonished congregation that, within a short time, "States goods" would be sold in the streets of Great Salt Lake City cheaper than in New York and that the people should be abundantly supplied with food and clothing.

"I don't believe a word of it," said Charles C. Rich; and he but voiced the sentiment of nine-tenths of those who had heard the astounding declaration.

Heber himself was startled at his own words, as soon as the Spirit's force had abated and the "natural man" had reasserted himself. On resuming his seat, he remarked to the brethren that he was "afraid he had missed it this time." But they were not his own words, and He who had inspired them knew how to fulfill.

The occasion for the fulfillment of this remarkable prediction was the unexpected advent of the gold-hunters, on their way to California. The discovery of gold in that land had set on fire, as it were, the civilized world, and hundreds of richly laden trains now began pouring across the continent on their way to the new El Dorado. Salt Lake Valley became the resting place, or "half-way house" of the nation, and before the Saints had had time to recover from their surprise at Heber's temerity in making such a prophecy, the still more wonderful fulfillment was brought to their very doors. The gold-hunters were actuated by but one desire; to reach the Pacific Coast; the thirst for mammon having absorbed for the time all other sentiments and desires. Impatient at their slow progress, in order to lighten their loads, they threw away or "sold for a song" the valuable merchandise with which they had stored their wagons to cross the Plains. Their choice, blooded, though now jaded stock, they eagerly exchanged for the fresh mules and horses of the pioneers, and bartered off, at almost any sacrifice, dry goods, groceries, provisions, tools, clothing, etc., for the most primitive out-fits, with barely enough provisions to enable them to reach their journey's end. Thus, as the Prophet Heber had predicted, "States goods" were actually sold in the streets of Great Salt Lake City cheaper than they could have been purchased in the City of New York.

Referring to this incident, in a sermon, a few years later, Heber says:

"The Spirit of prophecy foresees future events. God does not bring to pass a thing because you say it shall be so, but because He designed it should be so, and it is the future purposes of the Almighty that the Prophet foresees. That is the way I prophesy, but I have predicted things I did not foresee, and did not believe anybody else did, but I have said it, and it came to pass even more abundantly that I predicted; and that was with regard to the future situation of the people who first came into this valley. Nearly every man was dressed in skins, and we were all poor, destitute, and distressed, yet we all felt well. I said, 'it will be but a little while, brethren, before you shall have food and raiment in abundance, and shall buy it cheaper than it can be bought in the cities of the United States.' I did not know there were any gentiles coming here, I never thought of such a thing; but after I spoke it I thought I must be mistaken this time. Brother Rich remarked at the time, 'I do not believe a word of it.' And neither did I; but, to the astonishment and joy of the Saints, it came to pass just as I had spoken it, only more abundantly. The Lord led me right, but I did not know it.

"I have heard Joseph say many times, that he was much tempted about the revelations the Lord gave through him—it seemed to be so impossible for them to be fulfilled. I do not profess to be a Prophet; but I know that every man and woman can be, if they live for it."

Whitney, *Life of Heber C. Kimball* (Bookcraft), pp. 388-92.

HEBER C. KIMBALL

"Robert, Why Have You Been Complaining to the Lord?"

Robert Smith, a friend of Brother Kimball's and for many years almost a member of his family, says: "In 1857, I was working for Brother Heber and asked him for some goods which he refused to let me have. Feeling bad over it, I went home and laid the matter before the Lord. The next morning when I came to work, Brother Heber called me into his room and said, 'Robert, why have you been complaining to the Lord about his servant, Heber? Here are the things you asked me for and after this, don't go to the Lord about every little thing that happens.' "

President Kimball promised a brother that if he followed his instructions, he would be able to get a team and wagon. The man took him at his word and finally succeeded in getting a wagon and one horse, but he needed another horse so he reported to Brother Kimball that he had promised him a team, and that he had only one horse. Brother Kimball told this man to go down to his corral and get one of his horses, that he would have to help fulfill his own prophecy.

Hinckley, *The Faith of Our Pioneer Fathers*, p. 134.

Biographical Sketch

PRESIDENT ANTHON H. LUND

Anthon H. Lund was born in Aalborg, Denmark, on May 14, 1844. His father was a soldier and his mother passed on at a very early age, leaving him in his grandmother's care.

His grandmother was baptized in 1853. Anthon was baptized on May 15, 1856. In 1862 he moved from Denmark to Utah. While on the ship en route to the United States he was appointed physician. He arrived in Salt Lake on September 23, 1862, after being en route seventy-one days.

In 1870 Anthon married Sarah Ann Petersen, who was the daughter of a bishop. Together they had nine children who became very successful. Anthon was greatly respected and loved in his home as well as in the church and community.

In 1874 he served on the high council at Sanpete; in 1877 he was the stake clerk and member of the high council as well as being superintendent of the Sunday School in 1878.

Anthon returned to Denmark as mission president there. He stayed there two years and three months and upon returning to Utah he was elected to the territorial legislature and reelected the following term. He worked with establishment of the Utah State Agricultural College while holding this position.

In 1888 he became the vice-president of the Manti Temple under President Wells; in 1889 he became an apostle and in 1891 president of the Manti Temple.

Between the years 1893 and 1896 he presided over the European Mission.

In 1897 Anthon H. Lund visited the Orient with F. F. Hintze to reorganize the Turkish Mission.

In 1899 he was made Church Historian. He was the Sunday School Superintendent until 1919. In 1910 he was sustained second counselor in the First Presidency under President Joseph F. Smith. He also served as first counselor to President Heber J. Grant.

In 1911 President Lund became acting president of the Salt Lake Temple. In 1918 he was appointed president of the Salt Lake Temple.

He died on March 2, 1921, in Salt Lake City.

ANTHON H. LUND

"What a Delightful Day I Can Have Reading the Bible"

At the early age of four years Anthon H. Lund was sent to a private school, where he mastered the first elements of reading, writing, arithmetic, etc., and when seven years old he entered the public school of the city of Aalborg. His industry as a student and his aptitude for learning are shown in the fact that he rapidly advanced from one grade to another, passing entirely over the second grade. And while preparing himself for graduation in the course of study given in the school, he took besides private lessons in English, and also studied German and French. At the age of eleven years he held the first place in the school. Already at his early age Brother Lund had an irresistible desire to study the word of God. In his grandmother's house was a Bible belonging to his uncle, which his uncle had forbidden him to touch for fear he should soil or otherwise deface the precious volume. But his grandmother often asked him to read the whole book, and encouraged in this by his grandmother, he commenced at the beginning and made himself familiar with the main events narrated in that sacred volume. One day in Lent when the streets were filled with people looking at the Lent procession, he thought: What a delightful day I can have reading the Bible! He imagined that his uncle would be among the sight-seeing multitude. He had settled himself down on his favorite place with the Bible open, reading the fascinating history of Israel under the kings, when he heard a step on the stairs; the door opened and there stood his uncle before him. He asked his uncle to excuse his having taken the Bible without permission. His uncle answered: "I am delighted, my boy, to find you thus employed on a day like this. Read it as much as you like." As he was only in his eighth year, his uncle was surprised to find how much he had read, and how well he had grasped the meaning. Brother Lund said those early readings have been a great help to him, as they fastened the thread of the Bible narrative securely upon his mind.

J. M. Sjodahl, "Memorial Address of Funeral Service of Anthon H. Lund" (J. Reuben Clark Library, Brigham Young University, Provo, Utah), pp. 5-6.

ANTHON H. LUND

"Brother Lund Was Thirteen Years Old"

When Brother Lund was thirteen years old he was called to labor in the vineyard. His mission was to teach emigrating Saints English, to distribute tracts and help the Elders hold meetings. When giving his first report at the conference, Brother Fjeldsted lifted him upon a table, and thus he made his debut before an audience.

Besides his tracts, he always carried a number of the *Millennial Stars*, which he would read to the Saints, he being able to translate them into Danish nearly as fluently as if he were reading a Danish paper. The Saints were delighted to listen and were strengthened in their faith. A series of articles published in the *Millennial Star*, "Answers to Objections," was a great help to him in meeting the arguments of the ministers, who were then publishing in Danish the same falsehoods about the "Mormons," which had flooded America and England. When he was first sent out some thought the "Mormons" were going daft in sending one so young. Such a remark was once reported to Brother Lund. He said: "Never mind, I will make that man my friend." He did so, for in the course of time the man who had spoken so slightingly of him asked to be baptized and wanted Brother Lund to perform the ordinance.

Sjodahl, "Memorial Address of Funeral Service of Anthon H. Lund," pp. 9-10.

ANTHON H. LUND

"She Grabbed Her Firetongs and Screamed"

It was not often Brother Lund was molested. Even in places where other Elders had suffered persecution, he succeeded in making friends. Sometimes, however, he also tasted the opposite. On one occasion, when he was out inviting people to a meeting in the evening, he came into a house and informed a woman he met that there would be a meeting that evening, and invited her to attend.

"What kind of a meeting?" she asked.

"A 'Mormon' meeting," he replied.

There came a change over her face instantly and she became a perfect fury. She grabbed her firetongs and screamed, "I will give you 'Mormon' meeting!" and flew at him.

He thought discretion the better part of valor, and ran out of the house, but the woman followed, and in her highest key called on her husband to shoot the "Mormon." She made such a disturbance that the neighbors came running to see what was the matter.

Years afterwards, when Brother Lund had charge of the Ephraim Co-op, a lady came into the store and said to him, "You do not know me, but I have seen you once. Do you remember a woman who ran after you with a pair of fire-tongs?"

"Yes," he answered, "but you are not that woman, for her face I have never forgotten."

"No," she said, "I was her neighbor, and seeing her running after you, I asked her what you had done. She said that you had invited her to a 'Mormon' meeting. I became curious to learn something about the 'Mormons' and went to the meeting. I heard you speak and was convinced of the truth."

Sjodahl, "Memorial Address of Funeral Service of Anthon H. Lund," pp. 11-12.

ANTHON H. LUND

"Fists Like Sledge Hammers"

Brother Lund had on one occasion obtained permission to hold a meeting in a town where it had hitherto been impossible to make an opening. The meeting was appointed for the next Sunday; and in company with a couple of Elders, Brother Lund went there. On entering the town they were warned not to go to the meeting, as the mob would disturb the meeting, and they had given the blacksmith, the bully

138

of several parishes, all the liquor he would drink in order to get him to pound the "Mormon" Elders. They thanked their informant, but said they must honor their appointment. They found the house full of people and great numbers outside that could not get in. The meeting was opened, and in stalked the blacksmith. Brother Lund said when he saw him, he thought he was a very Polyphemus. He had only one eye, a sinister look, and fists like sledge hammers. They prayed earnestly that God would overrule the plans of the wicked. The advent of the blacksmith was the signal for disturbing the meeting and some commenced calling the Elders liars, etc. The blacksmith arose to his feet when he heard the interruptions, and slowly eyeing the audience he said: "I want you all to understand that these are men of God, and they speak his word pure and simple. If any one again interrupts them he shall feel the weight of this," showing his large fist. The crowd did not know what this meant; he had drunk their liquor and promised to thrash the Elders; he must be joking. A loudmouthed fellow commenced again calling the Elders opprobrious names, when the blacksmith elbowed his way through the dense crowd, and taking hold of the disturber he threw him out of the door. This settled it. For two hours the Elders preached to the congregation and the one-eyed giant stood guard as a policeman; but as soon as the meeting was dismissed, he seemed to realize that he was on the wrong side, and he commenced to be ugly and wanted to quarrel with the brethren, but they got away as quickly as possible. Brother Lund was the last to leave, and he heard those behind say to those in front of him, "Give him a diff!" But Brother Lund nodded politely to the crowd as he passed through and got away unhurt. Some of those present have since come to Utah and have informed Brother Lund that even the man who opened his house for the meeting was in the conspiracy against the Elders. The Elders felt that their prayers were heard in an almost miraculous manner.

Sjodahl, "Memorial Address at Funeral Services of Anthon H. Lund," pp. 12-13.

"I Will Make You My Heir"

One day while he was out tracting, he visited a large mill-owner, whom he found in his library with another gentleman. After spending an hour in answering their questions, the man of the house said: "It is too bad that you are a 'Mormon.' If you will study theology at the University of Copenhagen and become a Lutheran minister I will pay the expenses and I will make you my heir."

Brother Lund answered, "I have no doubt you are a rich man, but you have not money enough to buy my allegiance to the Church of God." The answer seemed to please both the gentlemen. Brother Lund has wondered since whether the man meant what he said or not. He believed at the time that he was in earnest, but it was not temptation to him. He felt he had found the pearl of great price.

His experiences in the mission field were varied and interesting. Once he had promised to meet at a certain place to help hold a meeting. To reach this place he walked some ten miles facing a heavy snow storm. When he arrived at the place he found the house full of people, but the Elders had not come. He sat down among the people and heard them say: "The 'Mormons' have fooled us today." When the time was up and he saw no one else would be there, he arose and asked the people kindly to give him their attention. How astonished the people looked at the boy! But they were so still that you could hear a pin drop. After the meeting every one present came and shook hands with him and thanked him. Several of those present have since joined the Church and emigrated to Zion.

Sjodahl, "Memorial Address at Funeral Services of Anthon H. Lund," pp. 10-11.

"The Physician of the Company"

At the age of sixteen he was ordained an Elder and appointed president of the Aalborg branch and traveling Elder in five other branches. This was at the time quite a responsible position, the branch being large and requiring constant care.

Elder Lund continued his missionary labors until the year 1862, when, at the age of eighteen, he emigrated to Utah. He left Hamburg on the "Benjamin Franklin." While lying in that city, measles came aboard and made fearful ravages amongst the children. There was no doctor on board, and the captain would deliver the medicines and wine for the sick only on an order from a physician. Bishop C. A. Madsen laid the matter before the Saints, and they voted to appoint Brother Lund to be the physician of the company. He received the medicine chest and with it a book treating on common diseases and their cures. This he studied diligently and performed his duties so well that he gained the confidence of both the crew and the passengers. Brother Lund was always in demand. At times he had to hide so as to get the much-needed rest and sleep. This was rather remarkable for a doctor that had been given his diploma by popular vote instead of by a medical faculty.

Sjodahl, "Memorial Address of Funeral Service of Anthon H. Lund," pp. 13-14.

"The Name of Anthon H. Lund"

I can endorse most heartily all of the splendid tributes that have been paid today to President Anthon H. Lund. My association with him has been as intimate, I believe, as it is possible for mortal men to be associated together. He came int the Council of the Quorum of the Apostles at the time that Wilford Woodruff, George Q. Cannon and Joseph F. Smith were sustained as the First Presidency of the Church. Each of the remaining apostles, nine of them, and their counselor, Daniel H. Wells, were asked to write the names of three men upon slips of paper to send to the Presidency as to whom they would like to fill the vacancy caused by these three men being chosen to preside over the Church, and each and every one of those ten men, without consultation with each other, put the name of Anthon H. Lund on their slips of paper. From that day until today I have never heard a word, I have never seen an act, I know nothing either in public or private of the labors of Anthon H. Lund, but what has been worthy in every respect of a Latter-day Saint, worthy in every respect of a disciple or an apostle of the Lord Jesus Christ, to which office he was called. While I was in Japan President Lorenzo Snow passed away, and I said to my associates: "If President Joseph F. Smith shall choose as a counselor the wisest, the best informed, the most level-headed man, the one that in my judgement has the greatest fund of information and the most remarkable memory of any man in the Council of the Twelve Apostles to be one of his counselors, he will choose Anthon H. Lund;" and it is needless to say that I was delighted when the news came that Brother Lund had been chosen.

Heber J. Grant, "Memorial Address at Funeral Services of Anthon H. Lund," pp. 46-47.

Biographical Sketch

ELDER JOSEPH F. MERRILL

Elder Merrill was born August 24, 1868, at Richmond, Utah. He was the son of Marriner W. Merrill and Maria L. Kingsbury.

Elder Merrill received a Ph.D. from John Hopkins University in 1899. He was the director of the Utah School of Mines from 1897 to 1928 at the University of Utah. He was appointed Church Commissioner of Education in 1928.

From his childhood Joseph F. Merrill has been active in Church service. While attending the University of Michigan he presided over the branch there and on his return he was associated with Dr. Richard R. Lyman in the superintendency of the Young Men's Mutual Improvement Association of Salt Lake Stake. For eight years he was counselor to President Frank Y. Taylor of Granite Stake. He was ordained to the apostleship October 8, 1931.

Joseph Francis Merrill died February 3, 1952, at Salt Lake City.

The First Presidency said:

Another great stalwart in the defense of truth, has been called home— Elder Joseph F. Merrill, a member of the Quorum of the Twelve Apostles. For years he has fulfilled every call made upon him, never excusing, never shirking, never complaining. He has been a minuteman in the service of the Lord, ready to meet every appointment given to him, equally ready, in case of emergency, to meet the appointment given to another. . . .

His faith was great; his courage, unflinching; his ardor, never wavering. His was a great voice in behalf of righteousness. Over a long and active life, he gave his all in the service of the Lord. We shall greatly miss his earnest, devoted, never-failing effort in that work.

The Improvement Era, March 1952, p. 144.

JOSEPH F. MERRILL

"I Sprang From My Knees"

I was reared in a family where prayer, night and morning, was always the order. I have seen my father sometimes too busy to stop to eat his breakfast, but never too busy to kneel with his family in prayer before he left, to thank the Lord for the prospects of the day, for the rest of the night, and to ask his direction and help in the labors of the day. I was taught to pray at my mother's knee, and when I could say my own little prayers, I was taught that it was my prayer; it should be said in secret, or at least to myself.

So I knelt on one side of the bed, brother on the other side, every night. He never knew what I prayed for; certainly I did not know what he prayed for. But when I was about ten years of age, I began to pray for a special blessing. But I did not get an answer. Why? Father had taught us that there are three factors that must characterize every prayer that the Lord will answer: We must pray for real needs—and even grown-ups, he said, sometimes ask the Lord for things they do not get, because they ask foolishly—we must pray worthily, and we must pray with faith.

In answer to my first prayer, no answer came. The faith

was there, I felt, to the extent that I could exert it. The need was there, I felt certainly no doubt about that, but was the worthiness? I could always think of something, as I prayed night after night without an answer, that I had done that I should not have done, and so I continued to pray, feeling that when I could make myself worthy of an answer, I would get it.

It was after I had been praying nightly for five years that the whole family went, one Wednesday evening, in the month of February, into town and attended a Sunday School entertainment. My class rendered its number, followed by another that sang, and I remember some of the words of that song: "Keep on asking, God will answer by and by." To me that was a revelation. I kept on praying.

Some four years later, in the latter part of the month of August, 1887, in my nineteenth year, after I had been praying nightly for nine long years with all the earnestness of my soul for this special blessing, I was alone in the bedroom, and I said, half aloud, "O Father, wilt thou not hear me?" I was beginning to get discouraged.

Then brethren, something happened. The most glorious experience that I have received, came. In answer to my question I heard as distinctly as anything I ever heard in my life the short simple word: "Yes." Simultaneously my whole being, from the crown of my head to the soles of my feet, was filled with the most joyous feeling of elation, of peace and certainty that I could imagine a human being could experience. I sprang from my knees, and jumped as high as I could, and shouted: "O Father, I thank thee." At last an answer had come. I knew it.

Why did it not come before? I have thanked the Lord many times since that he withheld the answer. A few days after that, Father said to me: "Would you like to go to Salt Lake City and attend the University of Deseret?"—a secret wish of which I had said nothing. I had finished, the spring before, what is equivalent in this day to a junior high school course, nothing more in the town. I wanted to go on and now I could. And as it turned out, after graduating at the University of Deseret, I went east and completed nine years of work in the field of science in four of America's leading universities.

Had I gone without an answer to my prayers at that critical moment in my life I might have forgotten to pray. But I think that I am here today—I think that I have been preserved in the Church, perhaps, because the answer to my prayer came at that critical moment, since which time never has a day passed that I have forgotten to pray. And as long as memory lasts I cannot forget the thrilling experience of that night.

The Improvement Era, May 1944, p. 281, 348.

JOSEPH F. MERRILL

"Tears Began to Run Down One Boy's Face"

In the bishops' meeting last evening in this hall, Bishop M. O. Ashton told two stories that deeply impressed me. Each story was about a bishop and some boys. In the first one, a group of boys engaged in some Halloween pranks of a rather serious, provocative nature. The bishop secured the names of the boys and charged them to come to the sacrament meeting and publicly ask forgiveness for engaging in the pranks committed, on pain of excommunication for failure to do so. In consequence there are in that community today a number of families that grew up outside of the Church.

In the second case a group of boys and a bishop were involved. A wedding party was held at the bishop's home. A big freezer of ice cream waited on the back porch for the refreshment hour. When the ice cream was to be served, it was observed that the freezer was empty. Pondering over the matter the bishop decided to invite the guilty boys to an ice cream festival and provided two freezers of ice cream for the occasion. All the boys accepted the invitation. When the lads were seated at the feast, it was noticed that tears began to run down one boy's face. Soon all the other boys were in tears also. From among that group have come some of the finest leaders in their community.

Those were the factual stories told by Bishop Ashton. Hearing them I was reminded of section 121:39-41, Doctrine and Covenants, which reads as follows:

> We have learned by sad experience that it is the nature and disposition of almost all men, as soon as they get a little authority, as they suppose, they will immediately begin to exercise unrighteous dominion. Hence many are called but few are chosen. No power or influence can or ought to be maintained by virtue of the priesthood, only by persuasion, by long-suffering, by gentleness and meekness, and by love unfeigned.

The two bishops of the story were undoubtedly actuated by the best of motives. Not for a moment would I question that. But one bishop was wise and the other unwise. The thought in the mind of one was to use persuasion, long-suffering, gentleness, meekness, and love, so beautifully stated in the revelation quoted. In the case of the other bishop he seems to have acted impulsively. . . . He forgot the scriptural injunction found in the Doctrine and Covenants 64:9-10:

> Wherefore, I say unto you, that ye ought to forgive one another; for he that forgiveth not his brother his trespasses standeth condemned before the Lord; for there remaineth in him the greater sin. I, the Lord, will forgive whom I will forgive, but of you it is required to forgive all men.

The Improvement Era, May 1945, p. 249.

"I Experienced a Shock"

Some years ago I was appointed to go to one of the stakes and re-organize the stake presidency. I was to go alone. After the meeting I spoke to President Clark and said, "You are acquainted in that stake. Who would you suggest to be the new president?" He said that he had no suggestions. I said, "I don't know a single soul in that stake except a public school teacher and I know he isn't going to be the president because he is not valiant in the faith. What shall I do?" He told me to go out and fulfill my appointment.

I went to President McKay and said, "I know you are acquainted in that stake because I am going to release the president you installed ten years ago. Who do you suggest?" He told me he had no suggestions. What could I do? I was going out there unacquainted. Well in view of some previous experiences I had, I decided to send over to the Presiding Bishop's office and get a list of all the priesthood authorities in that stake. That list came to me a little later, and the holders of the priesthood occupying positions of more or less importance were all listed in the wards in which they lived and the wards were listed alphabetically. I spread that sheet out in front of me and locked the door. Then I got down on my knees and prayed. When I got half-way down I experienced something . . . as true as I stand here I experienced a shock.

For many years I have been in charge of the electrical laboratory at the University of Utah and if ever I went to the switchboard and wanted to know if a couple of the terminals were alive, if the power was O.K., I quickly passed my finger on one terminal and passed another finger over the other terminal and I experienced a shock. If I did I would know the terminals were alive. This was not dangerous because there was never enough power to make it so.

I experienced exactly that kind of a shock when my eyes fell upon a name. I looked more carefully and this revelation in these words were impressed upon my mind, not in words audibly spoken, but nevertheless just as indelible as if spoken in tones of thunder, "He is the man." . . .

With the feeling "He is the man" simultaneously came that feeling of peace, of knowledge. I actually knew, I felt I knew and with satisfaction I went out and I knew who was to be president of that stake. We admonished them to ask God for guidance. We asked them to send a silent prayer to heaven to help them to feel. Seventy-six of these slips came back and sixty-nine had the name written on them. The name of the man I knew to be president of the stake. I asked the president, "Is brother so and so here?" He told me that he was sitting in the back. That was the first time I had ever seen the man.

Well how may we know then that a revelation is divine? Through feeling. It may be scholars would say, "My, my emotion." Do we not get knowledge through feeling? If I had a headache wouldn't I know it? How else can we know it?

I once went to a doctor and said, "Three days ago I fell on my shoulder and something is wrong with it." He took some X-rays and told me to come back the next day. The next day he told me that there was nothing wrong and he swung my arm around. I said, "Doctor, you say nothing is wrong, but if I gave vent to my feeling I would scream. The pain you are causing is so great that I can hardly stand it." I know I had a pain. How did I know? Through feeling.

Joseph F. Merrill, "Characteristic Teachings of the Church," Assembly, Brigham Young University, November 5, 1946.

Biographical Sketch

ELDER MARRINER W. MERRILL

Elder Merrill was born September 25, 1823, in Sackville, New Brunswick, Canada, a son of Nathan Merrill and Sarah Ann Reynolds.

In 1853 Elder Merrill left Sackville for Salt Lake City.

In 1861 he was chosen bishop of the Richmond Ward in Cache Valley, a position he held for seventeen years. In 1879 he was ordained first counselor to President William B. Preston of the Cache Stake. During this time he was also very active in civic and business affairs. Then in 1884 he was called to be president of the newly constructed Logan Temple and remained in that position until his death on February 6, 1906. On October 7, 1889, he was ordained an apostle and became a member of the Council of the Twelve, which position he also occupied until his death. Because of unusual circumstances, Elder Merrill in 1899 was also selected as president of the Cache Stake, so that for a year and a half, until his release from this position in 1901, he was serving concurrently as a member of the Council of Twelve Apostles, a temple president, and a stake president —and still found time to supervise his many business enterprises.

Because of his great interest in education, Elder Merrill was appointed an early member of the Board of Trustees of the Brigham Young College at Logan, serving in this capacity for many years. In 1895 the Governor of Utah appointed him a member of the Utah State Agricultural College Board of Trustees, and he served on this board until 1900. He considered his activities in education as among his most important duties.

Elder Marriner Wood Merrill's life was one of absolute adherence to the fundamental truths of the gospel. His thrift, integrity, and fair dealings with his fellowmen gave him opportunities that could not otherwise have been acquired. His attitude of honesty toward personal or business affairs was the same as that toward religious affairs. He considered his religious callings first and others second, but all were discharged with a spirit of integrity and honor.

Dedicatory Program, Marriner Wood Merrill Hall, Brigham Young University, October 21, 1959.

MARRINER W. MERRILL

"One Frying Pan (Borrowed)"

On April 9, 1854, I moved with my wife to Brother James Henrie's house, a small log house with one room, where for the first time since I left Sackville, N.B., I felt like I had a home to go from and come to. I made a bedstead out of small round poles and succeeded in getting a rawhide, which I cut up in narrow strips three-fourths of an inch wide and stretched them around and across the pole bedstead as cords to put our straw bed on. Our household goods consisted of one pole bedstead, one baking skillet (borrowed), one frying pan (borrowed), my chest for a table, two 3-legged stools, two knives and forks, six small tin spoons, etc. But we were happy and felt like it was home. The Lord blessed us with health and we both worked early and late to provide ourselves with a home of our own.

Melvin Clarence Merrill, ed., *Utah Pioneer and Apostle Marriner Wood Merrill and His Family* (Deseret News Press, 1937), p. 35.

"Won't You Sell Me a Little Flour?"

In the year 1855 the grasshoppers first came to Utah and did great damage to crops. But owing to the advanced stage of the crops when they came considerable grain was saved, but not enough for bread for the people. And before the harvest in 1856 great suffering was experienced by many for bread. My crop being short in 1855 and only raising that year 49 bushels of wheat, and out of that paying my tithing, threshing, blacksmith bills, etc., I was left with only a few bushels for the year's bread—not enough to last us. On finding that I would be short of bread stuff I got lumber from the canyon and took 750 feet to Salt Lake City to trade for flour, but found that kind of a trade very difficult. I could sell my lumber for money in different places, but could not buy flour for money. I finally as the last resort for flour took my lumber to Superintendent Daniel H. Wells, then Superintendent of Public Works for the Church, and asked him if he would give me flour for it. I must here confess that I had but little hope or faith to get flour for my lumber, as the Church had many work hands depending on the Superintendent for bread, besides a great many old and infirm people who looked to that source for supplies.

But to my surprise, after Brother Wells asked a great many questions as to what I wanted with so much flour, he said, "Yes, I will take your lumber and give you flour for it." I did not expect to get much flour for my load of lumber, as flour was worth at that time $20 cash per 100 pounds, when it could be bought at all, as it was a rare thing to hear of any flour for sale. Hence when Brother Wells asked me what I wanted with so much flour for my family I could not understand him, as 150 pounds of flour was all I expected to get for my 750 feet of lumber, and in fact I had offered it for that many times during the day.

Brother Wells did not ask me how much flour I wanted for my load of lumber, but simply said to me: "Drive it over to the Temple Block and Brother Fordham will measure it for you." I had told Brother Wells that my father-in-law with a large family and many of my neighbors were also out of flour, and that I expected to divide what I got with them. On getting my lumber measured and a receipt from Brother Fordham, and finding that I had $30 worth, it being considered worth $4 per 100 feet, which was the market price at that time, I went back to the Store House (then Tithing Office) with a light heart and cheerful countenance expecting to get 150 pounds of flour to take home to my family and neighbors. When I handed the receipt to Brother Wells he looked at it for a moment, and that moment seemed a long time to me, for I expected to hear him say, "Can't hardly afford to give you all flour for your lumber, you must take some cash with it." But to my surprise he said: "Brother Hill, go and put Brother Merrill up 500 pounds of flour." Six dollars per 100 pounds was the Church price then and for many years afterwards, and two dollars per bushel for wheat. I felt like weeping for joy, but suppressed my feelings and said secretly: "God bless you, Brother Wells, for your kindness to me. . . ."

Getting my 500 pounds of flour stacked on the running gears of my wagon, I started homeward, it being 8 miles to where I then lived north of Salt Lake City. I was extremely glad when I passed beyond the limits of the city, as I was accosted at every block with: "Say, Brother, won't you sell me a little flour? I will give you $20 in gold for a hundred pounds", etc. I was almost sorry I did not stay in the Tithing Yard until it was dark so people could not see what I had on my wagon, as I had no blanket or quilt to cover it up. But I had to say sorrowfully, "No, Brother, (or Sister) I cannot peddle out this flour, it is all engaged."

When I arrived home we felt to thank the Lord for His kindness to us. And we did not feel selfish with our store of bread, for we divided it with our brethren and sisters around us, and fed all who came in and asked for bread. We did not sell one pound of the flour, but loaned it and gave it to the poor, etc. We let it go so freely that before our little crop came in or got ripe we found ourselves nearly out again. One day a poor Danish or Swedish Brother came along and asked for some bread to eat. My wife told him we had but little but she would divide with him. When she set a little bread and milk before him he blessed it in his own language. I happened to be in the house at the time and felt that the Lord was with that man, and that although he was almost destitute of clothing the power of God was with him. He left a sweet influence in the house and our flour was increased to us in a manner unknown and we never have wanted for bread. God will bless all persons who will feed and comfort the poor of His people, and all such will never want for bread. Thus the hand of the Lord was over us and we were enabled to pass through those scanty times and gain an experience that has been valuable in after years.

Merrill, *Utah Pioneer and Apostle Marriner Wood Merrill and His Family*, pp. 41-44.

MARRINER W. MERRILL

"A Remarkable Experience"

During the winter of 1855 and -56 I worked in North Mill Creek Canyon as I had done the previous winter. And in this connection I will here relate a circumstance that occurred with me that winter while working in the canyon. During the month of January, 1856, the weather was very cold, the temperature ranging 20 to 30 degrees below zero at times. On one occasion I found myself in the canyon alone, as it was so cold no one else cared to risk going out in the canyon that day. I was at that time hauling house logs, usually five to a load. After getting my logs cut and dragged down to the loading place I commenced loading them on my bob sled, one end on the sled and the small end to drag on the snow. I had the five logs lying side by side. The loading place being very slippery, I was as I thought very careful. But after getting the first one loaded on the sled I turned around to load another one. The one I had on the sled slipped off like it was shot out of a gun and struck me in the hollow of the legs and threw me forward on my face across the four logs lying on the ground, or ice.

In falling, my hand spike, which I had used in loading the first log, slipped out of my hand and out of my reach. And thus I found myself with my body lying face downwards across the four logs and the fifth log lying across my legs, and I was pinned to the ground with a heavy red pine log 10 inches through at the large end and 22 feet long lying across my legs. And there I was with no visible means to extricate myself and there was no aid at hand, as no one but myself was in the canyon that day. I made up my mind that I must freeze and die all alone in the mountains of Utah. Many serious thoughts passed through my mind, as you may imagine. In falling on the logs my breast and stomach were hurt and it was difficult for me to breathe. I did not conceive what to do under the trying ordeal, but concluded to ask the Lord to help me, which I did in earnest prayer. After calling upon the Lord for some time I began to make an effort to extricate myself but all in vain, as I could not move the log that was lying on me. I, however, continued my efforts until I was exhausted and lost all recollection of my situation.

And the first I remembered afterward I was one mile down the canyon sitting on my load of logs and the oxen going gently along. My overcoat by the side of me, and feeling very cold, I spoke to my oxen and stopped them and looked around in wonder and astonishment. Then I remembered being under the log at the loading place some time previous. But how long I was there I could not determine, but supposed about two hours, as I was two hours later getting home than usual. I looked at the load and found I had the five logs on the sled, three on the bottom and two on the top, nicely bound, my ax sticking in the top log, my whip lying on the load by my side, my sheepskin (with the wool on, which I used to sit on) also on the load and I sitting on it. I made an effort to get off the load and put on my overcoat but found I could not do it, as I was so sore in my legs and breast that it was with great difficulty that I could move at all.

I put my overcoat on in a sitting position as I was and wrapped it around my legs the best I could and started on down the canyon. My oxen being gentle and tractable and the road smooth and all down hill, I arrived home without difficulty. On arriving there I found my wife was anxiously waiting for me and quite uneasy about me, as I was so much later than usual. She . . . helped me into the house, placed me by the fireside and made me as comfortable as possible and took care of my team. I was confined to the house for some days before I could get around again.

Who it was that extricated me from under the log, loaded my sled, hitched my oxen to it, and placed me on it, I cannot say, as I do not now, or even then at the time, remember seeing any one, and I know for a surety no one was in the canyon that day but myself. Hence I give the Lord . . . credit for saving my life in extricating me from so perilous a situation.

Merrill, *Utah Pioneer and Apostle Marriner Wood Merrill and His Family,* pp. 44-46.

"The Granary of Cache Valley"

I recall another incident that was quite remarkable that I might mention. It seems that President Brigham Young was in your father's home, and he pointed over to where Lewiston now stands, and said: "Brother Merrill, this will be the granary of Cache Valley." He told Brother Merrill to call a man to go over to that place to preside. So he called Brother William H. Lewis to go there and be the Bishop. Brother Lewis went, but the wind blew and the sand piled up against the fences, and he came back and announced that he would not give his small farm in Richmond for the whole of Lewiston, and wanted to be released. Your father told him that the Prophet of the Lord had said that would be the granary of Cache Valley and suggested that he go back there and stay with it. Brother Lewis did so and later became one of the wealthy farmers of Cache Valley, and the Lewiston sugar factory has been one of the best and most successful that we ever built.

Merrill, *Utah Pioneer and Apostle Marriner Wood Merrill and His Family*, pp. 374-75.

"Bishop Merrill of Richmond"

When the Logan Temple was nearing completion in 1884, the First Presidency of the Church had the responsibility of choosing the man to become its President. Several prominent men in the Church were under consideration for the position, including the subject of this sketch. But because of some prejudiced misinformation and false reports sent in to headquarters at Salt Lake by someone either jealous of Marriner W. Merrill or opposed to him on other grounds, the Presiding Brethren had put him out of the picture. However, President John Taylor earnestly desired to be guided aright in the matter and select the right man and so he prayed fervently for inspiration. While doing so, a voice seemed to say that the man for the post was Bishop Merrill of Richmond. In view of all that he had heard, President Taylor was exceedingly unconvinced and could scarcely credit the inspiration he received. So he prayed on. Then there came the distinct and unmistakable impression of a voice, "Bishop Merrill of Richmond." And that settled it and he was chosen, and he filled that position with energy, enthusiasm, credit, distinction, and general satisfaction until his death in 1906. By his personal characteristics and experience he was admirably qualified for that important calling and he willingly devoted the rest of his life to the work and duties thus devolving upon him; and he did it in a notable spirit of love and service to his fellowmen.

Merrill, *Utah Pioneer and Apostle Marriner Wood Merrill and His Family,* pp. 78-79.

"We Will Not Stop It"

One occasion I heard the late Apostle Marriner W. Merrill, President of the Logan Temple, relate this extraordinary incident:

He was sitting in his office one morning, he said, when he noticed from the window a company of people coming up the hill to the Temple. As they entered the Temple grounds they presented rather a strange appearance. . . .

A little later a person unknown to Brother Merrill entered the room. Brother Merrill said to him: "Who are you and who are these people who have come up and taken possession of the Temple grounds unannounced?" He answered and said: "I am Satan and these are my people." Brother Merrill then said: "What do you want? Why have you come here?" Satan replied: "I don't like the work that is going on in this Temple and feel that it should be discontinued. Will you stop it?" Brother Merrill answered and said emphatically, "No, we will not stop it. The work must go on." "Since you refuse to stop it, I will tell you what I propose to do," the adversary said. "I will take these people, my followers and distribute them throughout this Temple district, and will instruct them to whisper in the ears of people, persuading them not to go to the Temple and thus bring about a cessation of your Temple work." Satan then withdrew.

The spirit of indifference to Temple work took possession of the people and very few came to the House of the Lord for a period after this incident. It is not to be wondered at that Satan, who is the enemy of all righteousness, is displeased with temple work.

N. B. Lundwall, *Temples of the Most High* (Bookcraft, 1952), p. 99.

"Father, You Are Mourning My Departure Unduly!"

Elder Merrill was a man of many interests. His business of farming, merchandising, milling, stockraising, dairying, etc., called for careful supervision and wise management. These latter tasks were largely entrusted to his older sons. His oldest son, and namesake, was the one upon whom he leaned most heavily. In the prime of his life this oldest son died. This loss Elder Merrill endured with great difficulty and much sorrow. In truth, it seemed that his son's departure caused him to mourn unduly.

Apostle Merrill presided over the Logan Temple. He frequently traveled by horse and carriage from Logan to Richmond where his families were located.

On one occasion soon after the death of his son, as he was returning to his home, he sat in his carriage so deeply lost in thought about his son that he was quite oblivious to things about him. He suddenly came into a state of awareness when his horse stopped in the road. As he looked up, his son stood in the road beside him. His son spoke to him and said, "Father, you are mourning my departure unduly! You are over concerned about my family (his son left a large family of small children) and their welfare. I have much work to do and your grieving gives me much concern. I am in a position to render effective service to my family. You should take comfort, for you know there is much work to be done here and it was necessary for me to be called. You know that the Lord doeth all things well." So saying the son departed.

After this experience Elder Merrill was comforted, for he realized that the death of his son was in keeping with God's will.

Hinckley, *The Faith of Our Pioneer Fathers*, pp. 182-83.

"Eight Dollars Per Ton Is a Fair Price"

The spring of 1901 was a late one following a long hard winter. Nearly everybody's hay stacks were gone and feed for farm animals was very scarce. The few who had hay to sell could demand almost any price and those whose cattle were suffering for the want of feed would have to pay the price. Marriner W. Merrill, having sold his young stock during the previous autumn, had a good supply of hay left on hand when winter was breaking and spring was at hand.

Several different men had approached him asking him to name a price on the entire lot, some 75 to 100 tons. It would have been to his advantage to sell the hay in one lot and to receive his money in one check. These men wanted to buy it and sell it in small lots at high prices to those who were urgently in need of it.

Brother Merrill, as everyone called him, appointed me as his agent[1] to sell the hay in small quantities to those who actually wanted to feed it to their own cattle and who would not buy it to resell at a profit. He said $8.00 per ton was a fair price and that it should be sold at that price. When it became known that the hay, first-class timothy, was offered at that price people came to get their load or two—the limit allowed to any one until all others in the community had had a chance to supply their immediate needs.

Then came, one at a time, several men who had hay to spare and said to me who was handling the Merrill hay, "Why sell so cheap? There is a distinct shortage of hay and we few who have a little to sell may as well get $12.00 to $15.00 per ton as not." The proposal was presented to Brother Merrill, who, after thinking for a moment, said, "Eight dollars per ton is a fair price. That gives me a reasonable profit for producing it and it is all that those who are short of feed can afford to pay.

Continue to sell it at $8.00. After mine is gone those who demand more may sell for whatever they can get."

[1]James W. Funk, Elder Merrill's son-in law.

Merrill, *Utah Pioneer and Apostle Marriner Wood Merrill and His Family*, pp. 350-51.

Biographical Sketch

President Moyle was born on April 22, 1889, at Salt Lake City, the son of James H. Moyle and Alice E. Dinwoodey. He married Alberta Wright on October 17, 1919, and they were blessed with two sons and four daughters.

Elder Moyle graduated from the University of Utah with a degree in mining engineering. He served a mission in Germany and remained in that country a fourth year to study geology at the University of Freberg. When he returned he studied law at the University of Utah and received a Doctor of Jurisprudence degree from the University of Chicago.

He was a professor of law at the University of Utah for twenty years. He organized several industrial companies. President Moyle was very prominent in civic affairs. He served as president of the Cottonwood Stake farm 1927 to 1937. He was a member of the original Church Welfare Committee.

Elder Moyle was called to the Council of the Twelve on April 6, 1947. He became second counselor in the First Presidency in 1959 and was asked by President McKay to be his first counselor in 1961. Henry Dinwoodey Moyle died on September 18, 1963, at Deer Park, Florida.

HENRY D. MOYLE

"I Was Once Again Seated Comfortably on My Pony"

When I was a young boy my father entrusted the family cow to my care, both at our home in the city as well as at our home in the mountains in the summer. My first trip from the city to the mountains with the cow was made on horseback. I had a wonderful Indian pony, jet black in color and round as a barrel. She had a beautiful thick long mane and tail. She was my pride and joy. For the most part I rode her bareback and took great delight in currying her regularly. I even fed her carrots to improve the shine of her hair and even kept her shod, whereas most of the ponies were ridden without shoes. Somehow or other as a boy I sensed that whatever I did to per-'fect the pony seemed to pay dividends, the pony did more for me.

Well, I could go on telling you of my experiences with this pony, but it is the leading of the cow from Salt Lake City to Brighton in Big Cottonwood Canyon that I started to tell you about. You know it can be hard work leading a cow by a rope attached to her halter with the other end wrapped around the horn of the saddle. It took most of the day to get the cow from Salt Lake City to the mouth of the canyon.

Around noon I stopped at a farm located on Highland Drive below Sugar House, now built upon with houses. I milked the cow to make traveling easier for her and fed the pony and the cow. The fresh warm milk tasted good with the sandwiches Mother had put in my saddlebag.

Toward evening as we neared the Spillett farm, the cow balked. I lost hold of the rope, and the cow took off up the hill in the thick scrub oak brush. I left my pony on the canyon road. I climbed into the brush to hunt the cow, but I could not find her, and it was getting darker all the time. When I felt I had done all I could to help myself, I knelt down to pray. I knew then that the Lord heard and answered our prayers when we did our part. I felt good when I stood up. I was not afraid any more. I walked a short distance up the hill and came upon an old irrigation ditch that was used to bring water from the canyon stream onto some high land west and north owned by the Green family. A short distance up the ditch I saw my cow hidden by the lower high bank of the ditch. After thanking the Lord for answering my prayer, I drove the cow ahead of me in the ditch until we came out into the clear. I tied the cow to a bush, and soon went down the canyon road until I was once again seated comfortably on my pony, thanks to the Lord.

If I were you I would pray and develop the gift within me of talking to the Lord and depending upon him to help me when his help is necessary. You will find throughout life he will always be there to help you. Without his help, we do not accomplish much. With his help there is nothing we cannot accomplish if we will.

The Improvement Era, February 1963, p. 119.

"I Saw the Faith of That Boy"

A little black-haired boy, not more than eight or nine years of age, came up to me after our meeting in Basel [Switzerland], and with fear and trembling he said he wanted to shake hands with me, and when he got hold of my hand, he looked up into my eyes with his big black eyes and he said, "Brother Moyle, would you come and administer to my father?"

When I went to that boy's home, I met a faithful mother, and an older brother. That mother threw her arms around me, and she said, "Brother Moyle, we have fasted and prayed, and especially this youngest son of mine, that he might have the courage that we older ones lacked to ask you to come to our home and bless our father who is so critically ill."

I tell you when I saw the faith of that boy, and the faith of that mother and of that son, and of the appreciation that they had for the priesthood of God, it touched my heart to the very core. It gave me a sense of humility I would like to keep all the days of my life. The Spirit of the Lord and his power were there present, and we blessed that good father and gave to that family the desires of their heart through the gift and power of our Heavenly Father.

The Improvement Era, June 1954, pp. 430-31.

"It Was My Privilege to Eat at That Man's Table"

I was very greatly impressed when President [George Albert] Smith became president of this Church. One of his early responsibilities as president was to attend a welfare meeting of the general committee on Friday morning. His conduct there was indicative of the life that he had lived, the service that he had rendered his people, the knowledge that he had of the individual members of this Church. That first morning a case came before us for his consideration. It was the application for assistance of a humble Saint. He had come from a country in Europe, had not been here long, unknown to most of us although some of us had labored as missionaries in that same country. In the presentation of his case we were just a little impersonal and had not particularly emphasized his name. But the mere mention of it caused President Smith to ask if that man was not a former resident of Berlin. And when we told him that he was, he said, "How can we refrain from giving consideration to his case? His generosity in the Church deserves our help. It was my privilege to eat at that man's table." We found out later that he and his family had saved of their earnings for a week and had little or nothing to eat for that week, practically fasted in order that they might have the means with which to spread what they thought was an appropriate dinner before a servant of God who had been sent into their midst, one of the Quorum of the Twelve, George Albert Smith. I tell you, his interest in the people of this Church individually can hardly be excelled. He was interested in the smallest details.

Henry D. Moyle, "A Tribute to President Smith," *The Improvement Era*, June 1951, p. 453.

Biographical Sketch

Orson Pratt was born September 19, 1811, at Hartford, New York, the son of Jared Pratt and Charity Dickinson. He was a younger brother of Apostle Parley P. Pratt.

Elder Pratt was baptized on September 19, 1830. He traveled two hundred miles to meet the Prophet Joseph Smith in Fayette, New York. He also became acquainted with the three witnesses at this time.

He was ordained an apostle on April 26, 1835, under the hands of Oliver Cowdery, David Whitmer, and Martin Harris. He was one of the original members of the Quorum of the Twelve in this dispensation. He was only twenty-three years old when he was chosen by the Lord. Elder Pratt served numerous missions for the Church. He was a brilliant scholar, writer, and teacher and an eloquent speaker.

Elder Orson Pratt died October 3, 1881, at Salt Lake City.

ORSON PRATT

"Two Hundred and Thirty Miles to
See the Prophet"

For about one year before I heard
of this Church, I had begun seriously in my own mind to inquire
after the Lord. I had sought him diligently—perhaps more so
than many others that professed to seek him. I was so earnest and
intent upon the subject of seeking the Lord, when I was about
eighteen years of age, and from that until I was nineteen, when
I heard this Gospel and received it, that I did not give myself the
necessary time to rest. Engaged in farming and labouring too
by the month, I took the privilege, while others had retired to
rest, to go out into the fields and wilderness, and there plead
with the Lord, hour after hour, that he would show me what to
do—that he would teach me the way of life, and inform and instruct my understanding. It is true I had attended, as many
others have done, various meetings of religious societies. I had
attended the Methodists, I had been to the Baptists, and had
visited the Presbyterian meetings. I had heard their doctrines
and had been earnestly urged by many to unite myself with them
as a member of their churches; but something whispered to not
do so. I remained, therefore, apart from all of them, praying

continually in my heart that the Lord would show me the right way.

I continued this for about one year; after which, two Elders of this Church came into the neighbourhood. I heard their doctrine, and believed it to be the ancient Gospel; and as soon as the sound penetrated my ears, I knew that if the Bible was true, their doctrine was true. They taught not only the ordinances, but the gifts and blessings promised the believers, and the authority necessary in the Church in order to administer the ordinances. All these things I received with gladness. Instead of feeling, as many do, a hatred against the principles, hoping they were not true, fearing and trembling lest they were, I rejoiced with great joy, believing that the ancient principles of the Gospel were restored to the earth—that the authority to preach it was also restored. I rejoiced that my ears were saluted with these good tidings while I was yet a youth, and in the day, too, of the early rising of the kingdom of God. I went forward and was baptized. I was the only individual baptized in that country to many years afterward. I immediately arranged my business and started off on a journey of two hundred and thirty miles to see the Prophet.

Journal of Discourses, vol. 7, pp. 177-78.

ORSON PRATT

"Whirling Around Instantly"

But I will pass over the first years of the organization of the Church and come down to the time when the Twelve were chosen. It was in the year 1835. In the preceding year a few of us, by commandment and revelation from God, went up to the State of Missouri in company with the Prophet Joseph Smith. By the direction of Joseph I was requested to stay in Clay County for a few months, to visit the Saints scattered through those regions, to preach to and comfort them, and to lay before them the manuscript revelations, for they were not then fully acquainted with all the revelations which had been given. After having accomplished this work, and proclaimed the gospel to many branches of the Church in the western part of Missouri, I returned again a thousand miles to the State of Ohio, preaching by the way, suffering much from the chills, and the fever and ague, while passing through those low sickly countries, wading swamps and sloughs, lying down on the prairies in the hot sun, fifteen or twenty miles from any habitation, and having a hearty shake of the ague, then a violent fever, thus wandering along for months before getting back to Kirtland, Ohio, where the Prophet lived. In the meantime, however, I build up some few branches of the Church, and then started for the capital of the State of Ohio—the city of Columbus. I entered the city, a stranger, on foot, and alone, not knowing that there was a Latter-day Saint within many miles, but, while passing along the crowded streets, I caught a glimpse of the countenance of a man who passed, and whirling around instantly, I went after him, and inquired of him if he knew whether there were any people called "Mormons" in the city of Columbus. Said he: "I am one of that people, and the only one that resides in the city." I looked upon this as a great marvel. "How is it," said I, "that here in this great and populous city, where hundreds are passing to and from, that I should be influenced to turn and accost the only Latter-day Saint residing here." I look upon it as a revelation, as a manifestation of the power of God in my behalf. He took me to his house, and, when there, presented me with a paper published by our people in Kirtland. In that paper I saw an advertisement, in which br. Pratt was requested to be at Kirtland on such a day and at such an hour, to attend meeting in the Temple, that he might be ready to take his departure with the Twelve who had been chosen. The day and hour designated were right at hand; the Twelve were chosen, and were soon to start on their first mission as a Council. I had been travelling among strangers for months, and had not seen the paper.

I saw that I had not time to reach Kirtland on foot, as I had been accustomed to travel, and consequently could not thus comply with the request; but, with a little assistance, I got into the very first stage that went out, and started post-haste for Kirtland, and landed at Willoughby, three miles from Kirtland, to which I travelled on foot reaching there on Sunday morning at the very hour appointed for the meeting, which I entered, valise in hand, not having had time to deposit it by the way. There I met with Joseph, Oliver Cowdery, David Whitmer, Martin Harris, and others of the witnesses of the Book of Mormon, besides several of the Twelve who had been chosen and ordained a short time previous. They were meeting on that day in order to be fully organized and qualified for their first mission as a council. And, strange to relate, it had been prophesied in that meeting, and in prior meetings, I would be there on that day. They had predicted this, although they had not heard of me for some time, and did not know where I was. They knew I had been in Missouri, and that I had started from there, several months before, but the Lord poured out the spirit of prophecy upon them, and they predicted I would be there at that meeting. When they saw me walk into the meeting, many of the Saints could scarcely believe their own eyes, the prediction was fulfilled before them so perfectly. I look at these things as miraculous manifestations of the Spirit of God.

Journal of Discourses, vol, 12, pp. 87-88.

"I Feel Very Weak"

I have been in the Church almost twenty-six years, lacking about four months, and I have endeavored to do some little good; but really when I look back upon the twenty-six years of my life, or nearly that, which I have spent in this Church, when I look back upon my feeble labors, and my feeble endeavors, they seem to have been very small.

And although I have travelled much, and preached much, and written much, and tried to do some little good, yet after all, when I compare that which I have done, with that which it seems to me I ought to have done, in days gone by, I feel very weak, and am anxious that I may not be taken from the earth, until I have done more.

Journal of Discourses, vol. 3, p. 306.

Biographical Sketch

ELDER PARLEY P. PRATT

Elder Pratt was born April 12, 1807, in Burlington, New York, the son of Jared and Chanty Pratt.

In 1830 he left his home in Ohio and traveled eastward where at the home of a Baptist deacon he first came in contact with the Book of Mormon. After reading the book he went to Palmyra to see the Prophet but Joseph was in Pennsylvania. He talked with Hyrum.

On September 1, 1830, he was baptized by Oliver Cowdery in the Seneca Lake. On the same day he was ordained an elder in a meeting held in the evening.

In 1830 Parley P. Pratt was called by the Lord together with Oliver Cowdery, Peter Whitmer, Jr., and Ziba Peterson to become the first missionaries to travel west of New York.

He and his companions traveled 1500 miles west preaching by the way. Arriving in Independence, Missouri, they commenced a mission among the Indians. They visited the tribes of Shawnees and Delawares, teaching them from the Book of Mormon.

Elder Pratt was among the first apostles chosen in this dispensation; he was ordained February 21, 1835, at Kirtland, Ohio. He was just twenty-seven years old.

He served a mission to Canada in 1836 and baptized John Taylor and many others.

Elder Pratt began the publication of the *Millennial Star* in England in 1840.

In 1847 he moved to Salt Lake. He assisted in forming a constitution of the Provisional Government of Deseret, and was elected a member of the Senate in the General Assembly; and was afterwards elected to the Legislative Council when Utah became a territory of the United States.

In 1851 he became the first missionary of the Church to South America.

Elder Pratt was a brilliant writer and poet and many of his books are still used extensively today.

He was killed May 13, 1857, at Van Buren, Arkansas.

PARLEY P. PRATT

"I Walked Awhile and Then Sat Down and Read Awhile"

There are some, I presume, in this congregation who . . . have not heard my testimony. I have been acquainted in this Church and connected with it, from the first year of its organization in the wilderness of western New York. It was organized on the 6th day of April, 1830, and I was baptized into it about the first of September following.

When I first became a member of this Church, one small room could have contained all the members there then were in the world, and that too without being crowded, for at that time I presume there were not fifty.

The first thing that attracted my attention towards this work was the Book of Mormon; I happened to see a copy of it. Some man nearly a stranger to it, and not particularly a believer in it, happened to get hold of a copy; he made mention of it to me, and gave me the privilege of coming to his house and reading it. This was at a place about a day's journey from the residence of Joseph Smith, the Prophet, and his father, and while I was returning to the work of my ministry; for I was then traveling and preaching, being connected with a society of people sometimes called Campbellites or Reformed Baptists.

I had diligently searched the scriptures, and prayed to God to open my mind that I might understand them; and he had poured His Spirit and understanding into my heart, so that I did understand the scriptures in a good degree, the letter of the Gospel, its forms and first principles in their truth, as they are written in the Bible. These things were opened to my mind, but the power, the gifts and the authority of the gospel I knew were lacking, and I did really expect that they would be restored, because I knew that the things that were predicted could never be fulfilled, until that power and that authority were restored. . . . All this I was looking for, and the Spirit seemed to whisper to my mind that I should see it in my day.

Under these circumstances, I was traveling to impart the light which I had to others, and while doing this I found as before stated, the Book of Mormon. I read it carefully and diligently, . . . as I read I was convinced that it was true, and the Spirit of the Lord came upon me while I read and enlightened my mind, convinced my judgment and riveted the truth upon my understanding, so that I knew that the book was true, just as well as a man knows the daylight from the dark night, or any other things that can be implanted in his understanding. I did not know it by any audible voice from heaven, by any ministration of an angel, by any open vision; but I knew it by the spirit of understanding in my heart, by the light that was in me. I knew it was true, because it was light and had come in fulfillment of the scriptures, and I bore testimony of its truth to the neighbors that came in during the first day that I sat reading it, at the house of an old Baptist deacon named Hamblin.

This same Spirit led me to inquire after and search out the translator, Joseph Smith; and I traveled on foot during the whole of a very hot day in August, blistering my feet, in order to go where I heard he lived; and at night I arrived in the neighborhood of the little village of Manchester, then in Ontario County, New York. On the way I overtook a man driving some cows, and inquired for Joseph Smith, the finder and translator of the Book of Mormon. He told me that he lived away off, something more than a hundred miles from there, in the State of Pennyslvania. I then inquired for the father of the Prophet, and he pointed to the house, but said that the old gentleman had gone on a journey to some distant place. After awhile, in conversation, the man told me that his name was Hyrum Smith, and that he was a brother to the Prophet Joseph. This was the first Latter-day Saint that I had ever seen. . . .

I attended to my appointments, and was back again the next morning to Brother Hyrum's. He made me a present of the Book of Mormon. . . . I walked awhile, and then sat down and read awhile, for it was not my mind to read the book through at once. I would read, and then read on. I was filled with joy and gladness, my spirit was made rich and I was made to realize, almost as vividly as if I had seen it myself, that the Lord Jesus Christ did appear in His own proper person, in His resurrected body, and minister to the people in America in ancient times. He had surely risen from the dead and ascended into heaven, and did come down on the American continent, in the land Bountiful. . . .

As before stated, I fulfilled my two appointments; crowds heard me and were interested, and solicited me to make more appointments. I told them that I would not, that I had a duty to perform for myself. I bid them farewell, and returned to Hyrum Smith, who took me to a place, about twenty-five miles off, in Seneca County, New York. He there introduced me to the Three Witnesses whose names appear at the beginning of the Book of Mormon, also to the Eight Witnesses. I conversed with Oliver Cowdery, one of the Three Witnesses, and on the next day we repaired to Seneca Lake, where I was baptized by Oliver Cowdery, then the second Apostle in this Church, and a man who had received the ministration of an angel, as you can learn by reading his testimony.

After being baptized, I was confirmed in a little meeting during the same day, was full of the Holy Ghost, and was ordained an Elder. This transpired on the first day of September, 1830, and from that day to this I have endeavored to magnify my calling, and to honor the priesthood which God has given. . . .

Preston Nibley, *Missionary Experiences* (Salt Lake City: Deseret News Press, 1942), pp. 12-18.

"The Dog Was Fast in Overtaking Me"

It was now October, 1830. A revelation had been given through the mouth of this Prophet, Seer and Translator, in which Elders Oliver Cowdery, Peter Whitmer, Ziba Peterson and myself were appointed to go into the wilderness, through the western States, and to the Indian territory. Making arrangements for my wife in the family of the Whitmers, we took leave of our friends and the church late in October, and started on foot. . . . We continued our journey, for about two hundred miles, and at length called on Mr. Rigdon, my former friend and instructor, in the Reformed Baptist Society. He received us cordially and entertained us with hospitality.

At length Mr. Rigdon and many others became convinced that they had no authority to minister in the ordinances of God; and that they had not been legally baptized and ordained. They, therefore, came forward and were baptized by us, and received the gift of the Holy Ghost by the laying on of hands, and prayed in the name of Jesus Christ. . . .

In two or three weeks from our arrival in the neighborhood with the news we had baptized one hundred and twenty-seven souls, and this number soon increased to one thousand. The disciples were filled with joy and gladness; while rage and lying was abundantly manifested by gainsayers; faith was strong, joy was great, and persecution heavy. . . .

We had stopped for the night at the house of Simeon Carter, by whom we were kindly received, and were in the act of reading to him and explaining the Book of Mormon, when there came a knock at the door, and an officer entered with a warrant from a magistrate by the name of Byington, to arrest me on a very frivolous charge. I dropped the Book of Mormon in Carter's house, and went with him some two miles, in a dark, muddy road; one of the brethren accompanied me. We arrived at the place of trial late in the evening; found false witnesses in attendance, and a Judge who boasted of his intention to thrust us into prison, for the purpose of testing the powers of our apostleship, as he called it; although I was only an Elder in the Church. The Judge boasting thus, and the witnesses being entirely false in their testimony, I concluded to make no defense, but to treat the whole matter with contempt.

I was soon ordered to prison, or to pay a sum of money which I had not in the world. It was now a late hour, and I was still retained in court tantalized, abused and urged to settle the matter. . . .

I then observed as follows: "May it please the court, I have one proposal to make for a final settlement of the things that seem to trouble you. It is this: if the witnesses who have given testimony in the case will repent of their false swearing, and the magistrate of his unjust and wicked judgment of his persecution, blackguardism and abuse, and all kneel down together, we will pray for you, that God might forgive you in these matters."

"My big bull dog pray for me," says the Judge.

"The devil help us," exclaimed another.

They now urged me for some time to pay the money; but got no further answer.

The court adjourned, and I was conducted to a public house over the way, and locked in till morning; the prison being some miles distant.

In the morning the officer appeared and took me to breakfast; this over, we sat waiting in the inn for all things to be ready to conduct me to prison. In the meantime my fellow travellers came past on their journey, and called to see me. I told them in an undertone to pursue their journey and leave me to manage my own affairs, promising to overtake them soon. They did so.

After sitting awhile by the fire in charge of the officer, I requested to step out. I walked out into the public square accompanied by him. Said I, "Mr. Peabody, are you good at a race?" "No," said he, "but my big bull dog is, and he has been trained to assist me in the office these several years; he will take any man down at my bidding." "Well, Mr. Peabody, you compelled me to go a mile, I have gone with you two miles. You have given me an opportunity to preach, sing, and have also entertained me with lodging and breakfast. I must now go on my journey; if you are good at a race you can accompany me. I thank you for all your kindness—good day, sir."

I then started on my journey, while he stood amazed and not able to step one foot before the other. Seeing this, I halted, turned to him and again invited him to a race. He still stood amazed. I then renewed my exertions, and soon increased my speed to something like that of a deer. He did not awake from his astonishment sufficiently to start in pursuit till I had gained, perhaps, two hundred yards. I had already leaped a fence, and was making my way through a field to the forest on the right of the road. He now came hallooing after me, and shouting to his dog to seize me. The dog, being one of the largest I ever saw, came close on my footsteps with all his fury; the officer behind still in pursuit, clapping his hands and hallooing, "stu-boy, stu-boy—take him—watch—lay hold of him, I say —down with him," and pointing his finger in the direction I was running. The dog was fast overtaking me, and in the act of leaping upon me, when, quick as lightning, the thought struck me, to assist the officer, in sending the dog with all fury to the forest a little distance before me. I pointed my finger in that direction, clapped my hands, and shouted in imitation of the officer. The dog hastened past me with redoubled speed towards the forest; being urged by the officer and myself, and both of us running in the same direction.

Gaining the forest, I soon lost sight of the officer and dog, and have not seen them since. I took a back course, crossed the road, took round into the wilderness, on the left, and made the road again in time to cross a bridge over Vermilion River, where I was hailed by half a dozen men, who had been anxiously waiting our arrival to that part of the country, and who urged me very earnestly to stop and preach. I told them that I could not then do it, for an officer was on my track. I passed on six miles further, through mud and rain, and overtook the brethren, and preached the same evening to a crowded audience, among whom we were well entertained.

The Book of Mormon, which I dropped at the house of Simeon Carter, when taken by the officer, was by these circumstances left with him. He read it with attention. It wrought deeply upon his mind, and he went fifty miles to the church we had left in Kirtland, and was there baptized and ordained an Elder. He then returned to his home and commenced to preach and baptize. A church of about sixty members was soon organized in the place where I had played such a trick of deception on the dog.

Parley P. Pratt, *Autobiography of Parley Parker Pratt* (Salt Lake City: Deseret Book Company, 1966), pp. 47-51.

PARLEY P. PRATT

"A Letter of Introduction to John Taylor"

It was now April; I had retired to rest one evening at an early hour, and was pondering my future course, when there came a knock at the door. I arose and opened it, when Elder Heber C. Kimball and others entered my house, and being filled with the spirit of prophecy, they blessed me and my wife, and prophesied as follows:

"Brother Parley, thy wife shall be healed from this hour, and shall bear a son, and his name shall be Parley; and he shall be a chosen instrument in the hands of the Lord to inherit the priesthood and to walk in the steps of his father. He shall do a great work in the earth in ministering the Word and teaching the children of men. Arise, therefore, and go forth in the ministry, nothing doubting. Take no thoughts for your debts, nor the necessaries of life, for the Lord will supply you with abundant means for all things.

"Thou shalt go to Upper Canada, even to the city of Toronto, the capital, and there thou shalt find a people prepared for the fulness of the gospel, and they shall receive thee, and thou shalt organize the Church among them, and it shall spread thence into the regions round about, and many shall be brought to the knowledge of the truth and shall be filled with joy; and from the things growing out of this mission, shall the fulness of the gospel spread into England, and cause a great work to be done in that land.

"You shall not only have means to deliver you from your present embarrassments, but you shall yet have riches. . . ."

This prophecy was the more marvelous, because being married near ten years we had never had any children; and for near six years my wife had been consumptive, and had been considered incurable. However, we called to mind the faith of Abraham of old, and judging Him faithful who had promised, we took courage.

I now began in earnest to prepare for the mission, and in a few days all was ready. I took an affectionate leave of my wife, mother and friends, and started for Canada in company with a brother Nickerson, who kindly offered to bear my expenses. After a long and tedious passage in a public coach (the roads being very bad and the lake not open), we arrived at the Falls of Niagara sometime in the month of April, 1836. . . .

Leaving the Falls we continued our journey for a day or two on foot, and as the Sabbath approached we halted in the neighborhood of Hamilton, and gave out two or three appointments for meetings. Brother Nickerson now left me to fill these appointments and passed on to his home, in a distant part of the province.

I preached to the people, and was kindly entertained till Monday morning, when I took leave and entered Hamilton, a flourishing town at the head of Lake Ontario; but my place of destination was Toronto, around on the north side of the lake. If I went by land I would have a circuitous route, muddy and tedious to go on foot. The lake had just opened, and steamers had commenced plying between the two places; two dollars would convey me to Toronto in a few hours, and save some days of laborious walking; but I was an entire stranger in Hamilton, and also in the province; and money I had none. Under these circumstances I pondered what I should do. I had many times received answers to prayer in such matters; but now it seemed hard to exercise faith, because I was among strangers and entirely unknown. The Spirit seemed to whisper to me to try the Lord, and see if anything was too hard for him, that I might know and trust Him under all circumstances. I retired to a secret place in a forest and prayed to the Lord for money to enable me to cross the lake. I then entered Hamilton and commenced to chat with some of the people. I had not tarried many minutes before I was accosted by a stranger, who inquired my name and where I was going. He also asked me if I did not want some money. I said yes. He then gave me ten dollars and a letter of introduction to John Taylor, of Toronto where I arrived the same evening.

Mrs. Taylor received me kindly, and went for her husband, who was busy in his mechanic shop. To them I made known my errand to the city. . . .

Autobiography of Parley Parker Pratt, pp. 130-31, 134-35.

"She Threw Off Her Bandages"

In the morning I commenced a regular visit to each of the clergy of the place, introducing myself and my errand. I was absolutely refused hospitality, and denied the opportunity of preaching in any of their houses or congregations. Rather an unpromising beginning, thought I, considering the prophecies on my head concerning Toronto. However, nothing daunted, I applied to the Sheriff for the use of the Court House, and then to the authorities for a public room in the market place; but with no better success. What could I do more? I had exhausted my influence and power without effect. I now repaired to a pine grove just out of the town, and, kneeling down, called on the Lord, bearing testimony of my unsuccessful exertions; my inability to open the way; at the same time asking Him in the name of Jesus to open an effectual door for His servant to fulfill his mission in that place.

I then arose and again entered the town, and going to the house of John Taylor, had placed my hand on my baggage to depart from a place where I could do no good, when a few inquiries on the part of Mr. Taylor, inspired by a degree of curiosity or of anxiety, caused a few moments delay, during which a lady by the name of Walton entered the house, and, being an acquaintance of Mrs. Taylor's, was soon engaged in conversation with her in an adjoining room. I overheard the following:

"Mrs. Walton, I am glad to see you; there is a gentleman here from the United States who says the Lord sent him to this city to preach the gospel. He has applied in vain to the clergy and to the various authorities for opportunity to fulfil his mission, and is now about to leave the place. He may be a man of God; I am sorry to have him depart."

"Indeed!" said the lady; "well, I now understand the feelings and spirit which brought me to your house at this time. I have been busy over the wash tub and too weary to take a walk; but I felt impressed to walk out. I then thought I would make a call on my sister, the other side of town; but passing your door, the Spirit bade me go in; but I said to myself, I will go in when I return; but the Spirit said: 'go in now.' I accordingly came in, and I am thankful that I did so. Tell the stranger he is welcome to my house. I am a widow; but I have a spare room and bed, and food in plenty. He shall have a home at my house, and two large rooms to preach in just when he pleases. Tell him I will send my son John over to pilot him to my house, while I go and gather my relatives and friends to come in this very evening and hear him talk; for I feel by the Spirit that he is a man sent by the Lord with a message which will do us good."

The evening found me quietly seated at her house, in the midst of a number of listeners, who were seated around a large work table in her parlor, and deeply interested in the conversation. . . .

After conversing with these interesting persons till a late hour, we retired to rest. Next day Mrs. Walton requested me to call on a friend of hers, who was also a widow in deep affliction, being totally blind with inflammation in the eyes; she had suffered extreme pain for several months and had also been reduced to want, having four little children to support. She had lost her husband, of cholera, two years before, and had sustained herself and family by teaching school until deprived of sight, since which she had been dependent on the Methodist society; herself and children being then a public charge. Mrs. Walton sent her little daughter of twelve years old to show me the way. I called on the poor blind widow and helpless orphans, and found them in a dark and gloomy apartment, rendered more so by having every ray of light obscured to prevent its painful effects on her eyes. I related to her the circumstances of my mission, and she believed the same. I laid my hands upon her in the name of Jesus Christ, and said unto her, "your eyes shall be well from this very hour." She threw off her bandages;

opened her house to the light; dressed hersef, and walking
with open eyes, came to the meeting that same evening at
sister Walton's, with eyes as well and as bright as any other
person's.

Autobiography of Parley Parker Pratt, pp. 134-38.

PARLEY P. PRATT

"He May Be a Man of God"

Mrs. Walton expressed her willingness to open her house for Elder Pratt to preach in and proposed to lodge and feed him. Here at last was an opening. He began holding meetings at Mrs. Walton's, and was soon afterwards introduced to the investigation meetings held by Mr. Taylor and his religious friends.

They were delighted with his preaching. He taught them faith in God, and in Jesus Christ; called upon them to repent of their sins and to be baptized in the likeness of Christ's burial, for the remission of them; and promised them the Holy Ghost through the laying on of hands, together with a full enjoyment of all its gifts and blessings. All this, and much more that he taught, was in strict harmony with what they themselves believed; but what he had to say about Joseph Smith and the Book of Mormon perplexed a great many, and some of their members even refused to investigate the Book of Mormon, or examine the claims of Apostle Pratt to having divine authority to preach the gospel and administer in the ordinances thereof.

It was at this juncture that the noble independence and boldness of spirit, so conspicuous in John Taylor throughout his life, asserted itself. He addressed the assembly to the following effect:

"We are here, ostensibly in search of truth. Hitherto we have fully investigated other creeds and doctrines and proven them false. Why should we fear to investigate Mormonism? This gentleman, Mr. Pratt, has brought to us many doctrines that correspond with our own views. We have endured a great deal and made many sacrifices for our religious convictions. We have prayed to God to send us a messenger, if he has a true church on earth. Mr. Pratt has come to us under circumstances that are peculiar; and there is one thing that commends him to our consideration; he has come amongst us without purse or scrip, as the ancient apostles traveled; and none of us are able to refute his doctrine by scripture or logic. I desire to investigate his doctrines and claims to authority, and shall be very glad if some of my friends will unite with me in this investigation. But if no one will unite with me, be assured I shall make the investigation alone. If I find his religion true, I shall accept it, no matter what the consequences may be; and if false, then I shall expose it."

After this, John Taylor began the investigation of Mormonism in earnest. He wrote down eight sermons which Apostle Pratt preached and compared them with the scripture. He also investigated the evidences of the divine authenticity of the Book of Mormon and the Doctrine and Covenants. "I made a regular business of it for three weeks," he says, "and followed Brother Parley from place to place." The result of his thorough investigation was conviction; and on the 9th of May, 1836, he and his wife were baptized.

Leon R. Hartshorn, *Classic Stories From the Lives of Our Prophets* (Salt Lake City: Deseret Book Company, 1971), pp. 70-71.

"She Promised to Try to Live"

In camp we were placed under a strong guard, and were without shelter during the night, lying on the ground in the open air, in the midst of a great rain. The guards during the whole night kept up a constant tirade of mockery, and the most obscene blackguardism and abuse.[1] They blasphemed God; mocked Jesus Christ; swore the most dreadful oaths; taunted brother Joseph and others; demanded miracles; wanted signs, such as: "Come, Mr. Smith, show us an angel." "Give us one of your revelations." "Show us a miracle." "Come, there is one of your brethren here in camp whom we took prisoner yesterday in his own house, and knocked his brains out with his own rifle, which we found hanging over his fireplace; he lays speechless and dying; speak the word and heal him, and then we will all believe." "Or, if you are Apostles or men of God, deliver yourselves, and then we will be Mormons." Next would be a volley of oaths and blasphemies; then a tumultuous tirade of lewd boastings of having defiled virgins and wives by force, etc., much of which I dare not write; and, indeed, language would fail me to attempt more than a faint description. Thus passed this dreadful night, and before morning several other captives were added to our number, among whom was brother Amasa Lyman. . . .

We were now marched to Far West, under the conduct of the whole army; and while they halted in the public square, we were permitted to go with a guard for a change of linen and to take final leave of our families, in order to depart as prisoners to Jackson County, a distance of six miles.

This was the most trying scene of all. I went to my house, being guarded by two or three soldiers; the cold rain was pouring down without, and on entering my little cottage, there lay my wife sick of a fever, with which she had been for some time confined. At her breast was our son Nathan, an infant of three months, and by her side a little girl of five years. On the foot of the same bed lay a woman in travail, who had been driven from her house in the night, and had taken momentary shelter in my hut of ten feet square—my larger house having been torn down. I stepped to the bed; my wife burst into tears; I spoke a few words of comfort; telling her to try to live for my sake and the children's; and expressing a hope that we should meet again though years might separate us. She promised to try to live. I then embraced and kissed the little babes and departed.

Till now I had refrained from weeping; but, to be forced from so helpless a family, who were destitute of provisions and fuel, and deprived almost of shelter in a bleak prairie, with none to assist them, exposed to a lawless banditti who were utter strangers to humanity, and this at the approach of winter, was more than nature could well endure.

---

[1]The incident took place in Far West, Missouri, in 1838. *Autobiography of Parley Parker Pratt*, pp. 187-90.

PARLEY P. PRATT

"Go Free"

While thus sojourning as prisoners at large, I arose one morning when it was very snowy, and passed silently and unmolested out of the hotel, and as no one seemed to notice me, or call me in question, I thought I would try an experiment. I passed on eastward through the town; no one noticed me. I then took into the fields, still unobserved. After travelling a mile I entered a forest; all was gloomy silence, none were near, the heavens were darkened and obscured by falling snow, my track was covered behind me, and I was free. I knew the way to the States eastward very well, and there seemed nothing to prevent my pursuing my way thither; thoughts of freedom beat high in my bosom; wife, children, home, freedom, peace, and a land of law and order, all arose in my mind; I could go to other States, send for my family, make me a home and be happy.

On the other hand, I was a prisoner in a State where all law was at an end. I was liable to be shot down at any time without judge or jury. I was liable to be tried for my life by murderous assassins, who had already broken every oath of office and trampled on every principle of honor or even humanity. Hands already dripping with the blood of aged sires, and of helpless women and children, were reaching out for my destruction. The battle of Crooked River had already been construed into *murder* on the part of the brave patriots who there defended their lives and rescued their fellow citizens from kidnappers and land pirates, while the pirates themselves had been converted into loyal militia.

To go forward was freedom, to go backward was to be sent to General Clark, and be accused of the highest crimes, with murderers for judge, jury and executioners.

"Go Free!" whispered the tempter.

"No!" said I, "never while brother Joseph and his fellows are in the power of the enemy. What a storm of trouble, or even of death, it might subject them to."

I turned on my heel, retraced my steps, and entered the hotel ere they had missed me. As I shook the snow off my clothes the keeper and also brother Joseph inquired where I had been. I replied, "Just out for a little exercise." A walk for pleasure in such a storm gave rise to some pleasantries on their part, and there the matter ended.

There was one thing which buoyed up our spirits continually during our captivity: it was the remembrance of the word of the Lord to brother Joseph, saying, that our lives should all be given us during this captivity, and not one of them should be lost. I thought of this while in the wilderness vacillating whether to go or stay, and the thought struck me: *"He that will seek to save his life shall lose it; but he that will lose his life for my sake shall find it again, even life eternal."*

Autobiography of Parley Parker Pratt, pp. 196-97.

PARLEY P. PRATT

"Majesty I Have Seen But Once"

When we arrived in Richmond as prisoners there were some fifty others, mostly heads of families, who had been marched from Caldwell on foot (distance of 30 miles), and were now penned up in a cold, open, unfinished court house, in which situation they remained for some weeks, while their families were suffering severe privations. . . .

The Court of Inquiry now commenced, before Judge Austin A. King. This continued from the 11th to 28th of November, and our brethren, some fifty in number, were penned up in the cold, dreary court house. It was a very severe time of snow and winter weather, and we suffered much. During this time Elder Rigdon was taken very sick, from hardship and exposure, and finally lost his reason; but still he was kept in a miserable, noisy and cold room, and compelled to sleep on the floor with a chain and padlock round his ankle, and fastened to six others. Here he endured the constant noise and confusion of an unruly guard. . . .

These guards were composed generally of the most noisy, foul-mouthed, vulgar, disgraceful rabble that ever defiled the earth. While he lay in this situation his son-in-law, George W. Robinson, the only male member of his family, was chained by his side. Thus Mrs. Rigdon and her daughters were entirely destitute and unprotected. One of his daughters, Mrs. Robinson, a young and delicate female, with her little infant, came down to see her husband, and to comfort and take care of her father in his sickness. When she first entered the room, amid the clank of chains and the rattle of weapons, and cast her eyes on her sick and dejected parent and sorrow worn husband, she was speechless, and only gave vent to her feelings in a flood of tears. This faithful lady, with her little infant, continued by the side of her father till he recovered from his sickness, and till his fevered and disordered mind resumed its wonted powers.

In one of those tedious nights we had lain as if in sleep till the hour of midnight had passed, and our ears and hearts had been pained, while we had listened for hours to the obscene jests, the horrid oaths, the dreadful blasphemies and filthy language of our guards, Colonel Price at their head, as they recounted to each other their deeds of rapine, murder, robbery, etc., which they had committed among the *"Mormons"* while at Far West and vicinity. They even boasted of defiling by force wives, daughters and virgins, and of shooting or dashing out the brains of men, women and children.

I had listened till I became so disgusted, shocked, horrified, and so filled with the spirit of indignant justice that I could scarcely refrain from rising upon my feet and rebuking the guards; but had said nothing to Joseph, or any one else, although I lay next to him, and knew he was awake. On a sudden he arose to his feet, and spoke in a voice of thunder, or as the roaring lion, uttering, as near as I can recollect, the following words:

"SILENCE, ye fiends of the infernal pit. In the name of Jesus Christ I rebuke you, and command you to be still; I will not live another minute and hear such language. Cease such talk, or you or I die THIS INSTANT!"

He ceased to speak. He stood erect in terrible majesty.

Chained, and without a weapon; calm, unruffled and dignified as an angel, he looked upon the quailing guards, whose weapons were lowered or dropped to the ground; whose knees smote together, and who, shrinking into a corner, or crouching at his feet, begged his pardon, and remained quiet till a change of guards.

I have seen the ministers of justice, clothed in magisterial robes, and criminals arraigned before them, while life was suspended on a breath, in the Courts of England; I have witnessed a Congress in solemn session to give laws to nations; I have tried to conceive of kings, or royal courts, or thrones and crowns; and of emperors assembled to decide the fate of kingdoms; but dignity and majesty have I seen but *once*, as it stood in chains, at midnight, in a dungeon in an obscure village of Missouri.

***

Autobiography of Parley Parker Pratt, pp. 209-11.

PARLEY P. PRATT

"A Soft Hand Seemed Placed Within My Own"

Under these painful circumstances we spent a long and dreary winter. Our whole community, who were not in prison, were forced out of the State, with the loss of homes, property, and many lives. They fled by thousands to Illinois.

My wife visited me several times in prison; but at length the period expired that the State authorities had stipulated for every Mormon to be gone, and my wife and children, and a few others who remained behind were obliged to fly or be exterminated. . . .

To be tried without friends or witnesses, or even with them, by a set of "Gadianton robbers" and murderers, who could drive out and murder women and children, was but to be condemned and executed; to tarry there and drag out a miserable life, while our wives and children wandered abroad in a land of strangers, without the protection of husbands and fathers, was worse than to die ten thousand deaths.

Under these circumstances, and half way between hope and despair, I spent several days in fasting and prayer, during which one deep and all absorbing inquiry, one only thought, seemed to hold possession of my mind. It seemed to me that if there was a God in Heaven who ever spake to man on earth I would know from him the truth of this one question. It was not how long shall I suffer; it was not when or by what means I should be delivered; but it was simply this: Shall I ever, at any time, however distant it may be, or whatever I may suffer first; shall I ever be free again in this life, and enjoy the society of my dear wife and children, and walk abroad at liberty, dwell in society and preach the gospel, as I have done in bygone years?

Let me be sure of this and I care not what I suffer. To circumnavigate the globe, to traverse the deserets of Arabia, to wander amid the wild scenes of the Rocky Mountains to accomplish so desirable an object, would seem like a mere trifle if I could only be sure at last. After some days of prayer and fasting, and seeking the Lord on the subject, I retired to my bed in my lonely chamber at an early hour, and while the other prisoners and the guard were chatting and beguiling the lonesome hours in the upper apartment of the prison, I lay in silence, seeking and expecting an answer to my prayer, when suddenly I seemed carried away in the spirit, and no longer sensible to outward objects with which I was surrounded. A heaven of peace and calmness pervaded my bosom; a personage from the world of spirits stood before me with a smile of compassion in every look, and pity mingled with the tenderest love and sympathy in every expression of the countenance. A soft hand seemed placed within my own, and a glowing cheek was laid in tenderness and warmth upon mine. A well known voice saluted me, which I readily recognized as that of the wife of my youth, who had for near two years been sweetly sleeping where the wicked cease from troubling and the weary are at rest. I was made to realize that she was sent to commune with me, and answer my question.

Knowing this, I said to her in a most earnest and inquiring tone: "Shall I ever be at liberty again in this life and enjoy the society of my family and the Saints, and preach the gospel as I have done?" She answered definitely and unhesitatingly: "YES!" I then recollected that I had agreed to be satisfied with the knowledge of that one fact, but now I wanted more.

Said I: "Can you tell me how, or by what means, or when I shall escape?" She replied: "THAT THING IS NOT MADE KNOWN TO ME YET." I instantly felt that I had gone beyond my agreement and my faith in asking this last question, and that I must be contented at present with the answer to the first.

Her gentle spirit then saluted me and withdrew. I came to myself. The doleful noise of the guards, and the wrangling and angry words of the old apostate again grated on my ears, but Heaven and hope were in my soul.

Autobiography of Parley Parker Pratt, pp. 236-39.

PARLEY P. PRATT

"Liberty, Liberty"

We were finally to be removed one hundred miles down the country, and confined in the prison at Columbia, Boone County, to await a final trial.

A long, dreary winter and spring had now passed away, and the time drew near for our removal. We looked forward to the change with some degree of hope and expectation, for it could not be for the worse, and might, perhaps, be for the better. At any rate, the journey would give us a chance to leave our dark and loathsome dungeon, and look upon the light of day, the beauties of nature, and to breathe the untainted air. . . .

We arrived at Columbia, where we were immediately thrust into a gloomy dungeon filled with darkness, filth and cobwebs; the naked floor was our lodging. We had travelled hard, through rain and fatigue, for several days, and on the last day had rode till sundown without refreshment. We were extremely hungry and weary, but received no refreshment, not even a drink of water, till late in the evening, when our new keeper, Mr. John Scott, visited us with some buttermilk and bread; but we were now too much exhausted and too low spirited to eat. We thanked him for his kindness, and sank down exhausted on the floor, where we rested as well as we could till morning. . . .

After spending one night in our new dungeon we were called on by the Sheriff to come up into a more comfortable apartment, and were treated with some degree of humanity. . . .

My brother, Orson Pratt, also came to us with a firm impression that we were about to be delivered. He even predicted that we should go to Illinois. . . . He now began in earnest to make arrangements for our escape. . . .

Sundown, on the evening of the fourth [of July], was the moment agreed upon, and if we did not then appear they were to give us up for lost, and make the best of their way to Illinois and inform our friends that we had gone to Paradise in attempting to come to them. The reason for appointing this hour was this: Our door would be opened at sundown to hand in our supper, and we must then make the attempt as our only chance; for it was customary to lock us up in the lower dungeon as soon as the shades of evening began to appear.

This plan all matured . . . the fourth of July dawned upon us with hope and expectation. While the town and nation were alive with the bustle of preparation for the celebration of the

American Jubilee, and while guns were firing and music sounding without, our prison presented a scene of scarcely less life and cheerfulness; for we were also preparing to do proper honors to the day. We had prevailed on the keeper to furnish us with a long pole, on which to suspend a flag, and also some red strips of cloth. We then tore a shirt in pieces, and took the body of it for the ground work of a flag, forming with the red stripes of cloth an eagle and the word "Liberty," in large letters. This rude flag of red and white was suspended on the pole from the prison window, directly in front of the public square and court house, and composed one of the greatest attractions of the day. Hundreds of the people from the country, as well as villagers who were there at the celebration, would come up and stare at the flag, and reading the motto, would go swearing or laughing away, exclaiming, "Liberty! Liberty! What have the Mormons to do with celebrating *liberty* in a damned old prison?" . . .

The prison at Columbia was situated in the same square with the court house, being on the north edge of the town. Between it and the wilderness, where our friends held the horses in waiting, there were several fields and fences, say for the distance of half a mile, consisting of meadow and pasture land, and all in full view of the town. The prison consisted of a block house, two stories high, with two rooms below and two above. The keeper and his family occupied one end, and the other was used as the prison—the only entrance being through the lower room of the dwelling part, which was occupied by the family, and then up a steep flight of stairs, at the head of which was a heavy oaken door, ironed, locked and bolted as if to secure a Bonaparte or a Samson. On the inside of this was still another door, which was but slender, with a square hole near the top, of sufficient size to hand in the food and dishes of the prisoners.

The large, heavy door had always to be opened when food, drink, or other articles were handed in; and while open, the inner door served as a temporary guard to prevent prisoners from escaping, and was not always opened on such occasions . . . the food being handed through the hole in the top of the door, while the door itself remained locked. . . .

Now, our whole chance of escape depended on the question, whether the inner door would be opened that evening. . . .

As the sun began to decline behind the long range of forest which bounded the western horizon, and the lengthened shadows of the tall trees were thrown over our prison, we called upon the Lord to prosper us and open our way. . . .

The sun was now setting, and the footsteps of the old keeper were heard on the stairs—the key turned, the outer door grated on its huge hinges, while at the same moment we sprang upon our feet, hats and coats on . . . and stood by the door to act the part of waiters in receiving the dishes and food for supper. . . .

". . . It will be more convenient to unlock and hand it in at the door."

With this it was lowered down again, and the key turned on the inner door.

In this, as in most other fields of battle, where liberty and life depend on the issue, everyone understood the part assigned to him and exactly filled it. Mr. Follett was to give the door a sudden pull, and fling it wide open the moment the key was turned. Mr. Phelps being well-skilled in wrestling was to press out foremost, and come in contact with the jailer; I was to follow in the centre, and Mr. Follett, who held the door, was to bring up the rear, while Sister Phelps was to pray.

No sooner was the key turned than the door was seized by Mr. Follett with both hands; and with his foot placed against the wall, he soon opened a passage, which was in the same instant filled by Mr. Phelps, and followed by myself and Mr. Follett. . . .

By this time the town was all in motion. The quietness of the evening was suddenly changed into noise and bustle, and it was soon evident that the thrilling scenes of the great drama of the 4th of July, and of the Columbian celebration of liberty were yet to be enacted. The streets on both sides of the fields where we were running were soon thronged with soldiers in uniform, mounted riflemen, footmen with fence stakes, clubs, or with whatever came to hand, and with boys, dogs, etc., all running, rushing, screaming, swearing, shouting, bawling and looking, while clouds of dust rose behind them. . . .

As soon as the prisoners drew near, they were hailed by their friends, and conducted to the horses. . . .

I had taken about the third jump with my horse when I encountered a man rushing upon me with a rifle, and, taking aim at my head, he said, 'G-d d--n you, stop, or I'll shoot you." He was then only a few paces from me, and others were rushing close in his rear, but I turned my horse quickly in another direction, and rushed with all speed into the thickest of the forest, followed for some minutes by him and his dog; but I soon found myself alone, while I could only hear the sound of distant voices, the rushing of horsemen in every direction, with the barking of dogs. . . .

I now sat down in safety, and took a small biscuit from my pocket which sister Phelps had kindly provided, and which was my only store of food for the journey. With a hearty drink from the crystal stream and this biscuit I made my first breakfast, after my imprisonment, as a free son of Columbia. I recollect that while I sat enjoying this solitary meal, far from friends and home, surrounded with a scenery strange and wild, and without any guide or any knowledge where I should claim the next refreshment, I thought of the sweets of liberty I now enjoyed, and with a thankful and joyous heart I exclaimed loud, "Thank God for this hour, it is the happiest of my life; I am free, although lost in the wilderness, and if I cannot find myself, thank God nobody else can find me. . . ."

Autobiography of Parley Parker Pratt, pp. 239-56.

"In the Name of Jesus Christ, Arise and Walk"

We removed to Nauvoo, a new town, about fifty miles above Quincy. Here lived President Joseph Smith and many of the refugees who had survived the storm of persecution in Missouri. It had been already appointed as a gathering place for the scattered Saints, and many families were on the ground, living in the open air, or under the shade of trees, tents, wagons, etc. While others occupied a few old buildings, which they had purchased or rented. Others, again, were living in some old log buildings on the opposite side of the Mississippi, at a place called Montrose, and which had formerly served the purpose of barracks for soldiers.

The hardships and exposures consequent on the persecutions, caused a general sickness. Here and there, and in every place, a majority of the people were prostrated with malignant fevers, agues, etc.

When we first arrived we lived in the open air, without any other shelter whatever. Here I met brother Joseph Smith, from whom I had been separated since the close of the mock trial in Richmond the year previous. Neither of us could refrain from tears as we embraced each other once more as free men. We felt like shouting hosannah in the highest, and giving glory to that God who had delivered us in fulfilment of His Word to His servant Joseph the previous autumn, when we were being carried into captivity in Jackson County, Missouri. He blessed me with a warmth of sympathy and brotherly kindness which I shall never forget. Here also I met with Hyrum Smith and many others of my fellow prisoners with a glow of mutual joy and satisfaction which language will never reveal. Father and mother Smith, the parents of our Prophet and President, were also overwhelmed with tears of joy and congratulation; they wept like little children as they took me by the hand; but, O, how different from the tears of bitter sorrow which were pouring down their cheeks as they gave us the parting hand in Far West, and saw us dragged away by fiends in human form.

After the gush of feelings consequent on our happy meeting had subsided, I accompanied Joseph Smith over the Mississippi in a skiff to visit some friends in Montrose. Here many were lying sick and at the point of death. Among these was my old friend and fellow servant, Elijah Fordham, who had been with me in that extraordinary work in New York City in 1837. He was now in the last stage of a deadly fever. He lay prostrate and nearly speechless, with his feet poulticed; his eyes were sunk in their sockets; his flesh was gone; the paleness of death was upon him; and he was hardly to be distinguished from a corpse. His wife was weeping over him, and preparing clothes for his burial.

Brother Joseph took him by the hand, and in a voice and energy which would seemingly have raised the dead, he cried: "BROTHER FORDHAM, IN THE NAME OF JESUS CHRIST, ARISE AND WALK." It was a voice which could be heard from house to house and nearly through the neighborhood. It was like the roaring of a lion, or the heavy thunderbolt. Brother Fordham leaped from his dying bed in an instant, shook the poultices and bandages from his feet, put on his clothes so quick that none got a chance to assist him, and taking . . . a little refreshment, he walked us from house to house assisting other sick beds, and joining in prayer and ministrations for them, while the people followed us, and with joy and amazement gave glory to God. Several more were called up in a similar manner and were healed.

Autobiography of Parley Parker Pratt, pp. 290-94.

Biographical Sketch

ELDER FRANKLIN DEWEY RICHARDS

Elder Richards was born on April 2, 1821, at Richmond, Massachusetts, to Phinehar Richards and Wealthy Dewey. He was their fourth of nine children.

He was taught the gospel by two cousins, Brigham and Joseph Young, and was baptized in 1838 at the age of seventeen. In 1840 he was ordained a seventy and was called to his first mission. He led a company of Saints to the Salt Lake Valley in 1848. When he was twenty-eight years old he filled a vacancy in the Quorum of the Twelve. He was ordained an apostle February 12, 1849, by Heber C. Kimball. He served a mission in England in 1850. In 1854 he was called to preside over the European Mission. In 1866 he presided over the British Mission.

Elder Richards served for fourteen years as the probate judge of Weber County. In 1889 he became the Church Historian.

Elder Richards became the President of the Twelve on September 13, 1899.

He died at age 78 on December 9, 1899, at his home in Ogden, Utah.

FRANKLIN DEWEY RICHARDS

"One Potato for the Sick Child"

On June 10, 1846, Franklin wrote: I accepted the offer of two yoke of oxen, a wagon, a jack screw, a chain and a whip, the whole valued at not to exceed one hundred and twenty five dollars, in exchange for a two story brick house, and an acre of ground which my neighbors a year ago considered worth five hundred dollars. About sunset we bade adieu to our little home in Nauvoo.

After arriving in Sugar Creek, on July 3rd he committed his loved ones to the protecting care of Divine Providence and turned his face sadly yet resolutely toward the east, without money and scantily clothed, to make his way across continent and ocean into a strange land to fulfill a mission he was called to prior to the death of Joseph Smith.

Jane Snyder Richards started out for the west without her husband, and twenty days after leaving Sugar Creek she gave birth to her second child, a son whom she named Isaac; but the babe had barely opened its eyes upon this world when it was summoned to the spirit land. The picture of this homeless pilgrim mother, lying helpless in her wagon on the broad, lonely prairie, her dead babe on her breast, and her husband a thousand miles away, was pitiful enough to melt a heart of stone.

At this time her only remaining child, Wealthy, not yet three years old, was lying sick, having been stricken sick from a disease shortly after they left Sugar Creek. As they approached the Missouri River she gradually grew weaker and weaker. She had scarcely eaten anything for a month or more. She was very fond of potatoes, and one day while passing a farm in the midst of a fine field of these vegetables, hearing them mentioned, she asked for one. Jane Snyder Richards' mother went to the house to ask if they could have one potato for the sick child. "I wouldn't sell or give one of you Mormons a potato to save your life," was the woman's brutal reply. She had even set her dog upon Sister Snyder when she saw her approaching. Wealthy died on the 14th of September and was buried at Cutler's Park a little west of the Missouri River. The first night Brother Richards arrived in Liverpool he wrote: Today my little daughter Wealthy, if she lives, is three years old. May her life and health be precious in thy sight, O Lord.

Franklin L. West, *Life of Franklin D. Richards* (Salt Lake City: Deseret News Press, 1924), pp. 68-71.

FRANKLIN DEWEY RICHARDS

"Brother Brigham, I Always Have Accepted"

This morning I awoke from a dream in which I seemed to have been with President Brigham Young in the temple at Nauvoo. We sat opposite each other, with our feet in a clear, lively pool of water, and we conversed together. He asked, "Brother Franklin, would you accept it if I should appoint you one of the quorum?" I replied, "Brother Brigham, I always have accepted, and as far as I could, have obeyed every appointment that has been given to me, and I always intend to." He then showed me several books containing several peculiar drawings and diagrams, many of which were lightly colored and in the Prophet Joseph Smith's own hand writing. While I was examining the books I awoke, and felt as happy as if I had been really in the company of President Young and the holy influence seemed to rest upon my whole person.

This dream had its fulfillment two years later, when Franklin D. Richards was ordained an Apostle and called into the Quorum of the Twelve.

West, *Life of Franklin D. Richards*, pp. 81-82.

FRANKLIN DEWEY RICHARDS

"He and Brother Maeser Could Understand Each Other"

On the night of October 14, 1855, the three Elders (Franklin D. Richards, William Budge, and William H. Kimball), Dr. Maeser, Edward Schoenfeldt and some others, repaired to the banks of the historic Elbe, in which river Dr. Maeser was baptized by Apostle Richards. It was the first baptism in Saxony in this dispensation. After performing the baptism the party started back toward the home of Dr. Maeser. The only elder who could speak German was William Budge, and the conversation was carried on between Apostle Richards and Dr. Maeser, with Elder Budge acting as interpreter. The colloquy had not proceeded far, however, when Apostle Richards told Elder Budge that it was not necessary for him to interpret any more, as he and Brother Maeser could 'understand each other perfectly.' Brother Schoenfeldt relates that it was a very dark night, and when he first realized that the two men were conversing together with perfect facility, yet neither understood the native tongue of the other, his feelings were indescribable, for he knew that it was a divine manifestation. Dr. Maeser, in later years, testified that when he emerged from the water, he prayed that his faith might be confirmed by some manifestation from heaven, and he felt confident that his prayer would be answered.

Jenson, *LDS Biographical Encyclopedia*, p. 708.

FRANKLIN DEWEY RICHARDS

"With a Hand Over Each Ear"

Brother Richards' impression of a storm on the sea: The captain and his mate were both in waterproof suits, each with a speaking trumpet passing orders to the men. They could scarcely make themselves heard from one mast to another, so loud had the tempest now become. It was a scene of terrific grandeur, such as I had longed to behold. The winds, howling through the rigging, made music on as many different notes as there were ropes of different sizes and lengths, and seemed by their melody, to move the clouds in Jehu-like velocity, with their stirring strains. The sea seemed to catch the enthusiasm and become enwrapped in an ecstasy of joy. The winds and waves—two great forces of nature—seemed pleading with one another in awful tones of eloquence, as if contending for their respective rights to our gallant ship. Ever and anon 'Queen of the West' would mount the summit of a mighty billow, as if to bid adieu to the watery regions, and then descend as if destined for the bottom of the sea. Father Neptune won his case, and the effect upon the listener and beholder was no less powerful than sublime. I held on my hat, with a hand over each ear, to prevent ear-ache, and took my position on top of a lifeboat, gazing and listening with admiration and delight, until the powerful intonations of nature's great orators caused my head to throb with pain. I then retired to my room to spend the remainder of a Sabbath evening meditation upon the solemn and impressive divine service that I had just attended.

West, *Life of Franklin D. Richards*, pp. 68-71.

FRANKLIN DEWEY RICHARDS

"He Rebuked the Storm"

While on one of his trips across the Atlantic, returning from the British Mission in charge of a company of saints and Elders, the weather was very stormy, and the waves were rolling so high that the officers of the vessel were fearful of its being dashed to pieces. When the hearts of strong men were failing them, he remembered he held the holy Priesthood, which authorized him to rebuke the angry elements and command them to be still, as was done by the Savior and the Apostles in their day. Withdrawing to a part of the ship where he was unobserved, and raising his hands to high heaven, he rebuked the storm, the furious winds and waves, in the Name of the Lord Jesus Christ, commanding them to cease their violence and to be calm. The tempest immediately subsided; none of the passengers were lost, and no damage was done to the vessel.

West, *Life of Franklin D. Richards*, pp. 85-86.

Biographical Sketch

PRESIDENT GEORGE A. SMITH

George A. Smith was born on June 26, 1817, in the town of Potsdam, St. Lawrence County, New York. His father was John Smith, the brother of Joseph Smith, Sen., and his mother was Clarrissa Lyman. John and Clarrissa Smith christened their son George Albert Smith, but throughout his life George called himself George A. Smith.

When George A. was eleven years old, the family received a letter from Joseph Smith, Sen., relating an account of the visions and experiences of his cousin, Joseph Smith, Jun. It was not too long before his uncle, Joseph Smith, Sen., visited Potsdam with the recently translated Book of Mormon. George's mother was the first of the family to join the Church. In the spring of 1832, George's father, John Smith, was baptized a member of The Church of Jesus Christ of Latter-day Saints. George A. met his cousin, Joseph Smith, Jun., for the first time in 1832. He became a member of the Church on September 10, 1832.

On March 1, 1835, George A. Smith was ordained as the junior member of the First Quorum of Seventies. Three months later he left on his first mission to the eastern states.

George A. had been set apart to fulfill a mission to England

and he soon started on this important calling. At the age of twenty-one he was ordained an apostle, on April 26, 1839.

Brigham Young had called George A. Smith a "cabinet of history" and Orson Whitney had described him as a "walking encyclopedia of general information." Thus with this type of mind it was not surprising that he was called as Church Historian on April 7, 1854. He held this office for the next sixteen years.

George A. was sent as a delegate from the Territory of Utah in 1856 to go to Washington and request statehood for the territory.

In 1868 George's lifelong friend, Heber C. Kimball, died. In the October conference George A. Smith was called to be first counselor to President Brigham Young.

George Albert Smith died on September 1, 1875, at Salt Lake City.

GEORGE A. SMITH

"The Golden Bible"

In the month of August, my Uncle Joseph Smith[1] and his youngest son, Don Carlos, came to my father's on a visit and brought with them some Books of Mormon. My father had not seen his brother for about eighteen years and was delighted to see him. He had lived in Wayne and Ontario Counties, Western New York, a distance from us of two hundred and fifty miles. As my uncle was in a great haste to see his father, the next day my father took a horse and wagon and carried him to Stockholm, about twelve miles where my grandfather and uncles resided. My mother and myself occupied Saturday and Sunday reading the Book of Mormon; and on Sunday evening the neighbors gathered to see the "Golden Bible" as it was called by them, and commenced raising objections to it. Although I did not believe the book, their objections looked to me so slim and foolish, that I commenced answering them and expressed the fallacy of their objections so palpably, that they went away confounded.

I continued to read the Book of Mormon and framed in my mind a series of objections, which I supposed were sufficient to prove it false, and on the return of my Uncle Joseph, I undertook to argue with him upon the subject, but he so successfully removed my objections and enlightened my mind that I have never since ceased to advocate the divine authenticity of that book.

[1]Joseph Smith, Sr., the father of the prophet.

Zora Smith, *Ancestory Biography and Family of George H. Smith* (Provo: Brigham Young University Press, 1962), p. 44.

GEORGE A. SMITH

"I Cut the Ice in the Creek"

My father had been for several years very feeble in health and for about six months previous to his baptism had not been able to visit his barn. His neighbors all believed that baptism would kill him. I cut the ice in the creek and broke a road for forty rods, through the crust on two feet of snow, and the day was very cold. The neighbors looked on with astonishment, expecting to see him die in the water, but his health continued improving from that moment.

George A. Smith, "Memoirs," Brigham Young University library, p. 5.

"Keep Up Good Courage"

I undertook to study the Hebrew language under Professor Seixas, but failed for the want of eyesight. I was attacked with inflammatory rheumatism, which swelled my legs, right arm, and shoulder, so that I could not help myself for several weeks except with my left hand. I suffered the most excruciating pain, and although the winter was very cold, I could suffer no clothes on me except a very light blanket.

Cousin Joseph[1] came to see me. I told him I was almost discouraged, being afraid that my joints would be drawn out. He told me I should never get discouraged, whatever difficulties might surround me. If I were sunk into the lowest pit of Nova Scotia and all the Rocky Mountains piled on top of me, I ought not be discouraged, but hang on, exercise faith, and keep up good courage, and I should come out on the top of the heap. January 1, 1836, he laid hands on me in company with several of the Elders. My pain instantly left me and I gradually recovered my strength and the use of my limbs.

---

[1]The Prophet Joseph Smith.
Smith, "Memoirs," p. 49.

"The Minister Fled in Dismay"

A Lutheran minister arose when I was through, and stated that I had told the people that the Book of Mormon was true and they should all be damned if they did not believe it. "Now," says he, "we cannot be damned if we have not the evidence. As to the Bible its truth is attested in three ways. First, we have a map of all the country it describes. I challenge this stranger to present a map of Zarahemla spoken of in the Book of Mormon. Secondly, we have the original records of the Bible. I challenge these strangers to produce the original records of the Book of Mormon. Thirdly, we must have evidence that the translation of the Book of Mormon was rendered by competent persons. We demand these evidences. We are prepared to meet the issue. Our evidence is ready as far as the Bible is concerned, and the same evidence must be produced in relation to the Book of Mormon, or we pronounce it an imposition, and the propagators children of Hell."

In reply I stated that this gentleman could not be a man of fair reputation or he would not say in the presence of this congregation as he had said, that I had stated in my discourse that every one of you would be damned if you did not believe the Book of Mormon, when he must be aware that you all know that I said no such thing. Interrupting me he cried out: "Show the map of Zarahemla." I replied, "At any time and place that you will produce the map of the land of Nod, spoken of in Genesis, I am prepared to meet you and produce the map of Zarahemla." He said: "Show us the original plates of the Book of Mormon. I am prepared to exhibit the original of the Bible." I answered, "Any time you bring forward the original tablets of stone, upon which God wrote with his finger the Ten Commandments; and the original parchment of papyrus, upon which

Moses wrote the book of the law; and also bring the two sticks upon which Ezekiel wrote, I will exhibit the gold plates from which the Book of Mormon was translated."

The audience laughed, and the minister fled in dismay, cursing on his way.

Smith, "Memoirs," p. 49.

Biographical Sketch

ELDER REED SMOOT

Reed Smoot was born January 19, 1862, in Salt Lake City and grew up in Provo, Utah. His father, Abraham O. Smoot, was the second mayor of Salt Lake City, mayor of Provo, and one of the founding fathers of the Brigham Young Academy. His mother, Annie Kirstine Morrison, was a Norwegian convert who left her family to follow her newfound religion to Utah.

While in Salt Lake City, Reed Smoot attended schools under William Willes and Dr. Karl G. Maeser. In 1872 the family moved to Provo, where he attended the Timpanogos Branch of the University of Deseret. When the Brigham Young Academy opened in April 1876, Reed was the first student to enroll there. It is said that he passed through every higher course then offered, graduating in business and commerce in 1879.

The amazing business success of Reed Smoot began in the Provo Co-operative Institution where he was employed sacking produce, sorting potatoes, and doing odd jobs. Shortly after obtaining this position, he resolved that he would become superintendent of the Provo Co-op, a goal that he realized some 18 months later, in 1881.

After four years as superintendent of the co-op, where he made the business prosper, Reed became manager of the Provo Woolen Mills.

Already recognized as a successful businessman, Elder Smoot left home in November 1890 to serve in the European Mission.

In 1895 he was named as a counselor to Edward Partridge in the Utah Stake. In 1900 he was sustained as an apostle and set apart by President Lorenzo Snow.

In January 1903, the State Legislature elected him to the United States Senate. Elder Smoot served as a distinguished Senator for thirty years. The Senator from Utah could be cited as the one person most responsible for creating a favorable image for the Church.

Upon the Senator's return to Utah in 1933, he became an active member of the Quorum of the Twelve Apostles, but his health was already beginning to fail him. He served for 41 years as an apostle, his service ending with his death in February 1941.[1]

President J. Reuben Clark, Jr., paid Elder Smoot the following great compliment:

"I want to take this occasion to thank my Heavenly Father, as a member of this Church, for the return amongst us of one whom I regard as the greatest missionary of his own generation. I refer to the Honorable Reed Smoot.

"I went East to live at about the time he went into the Senate. I know something of the feeling that then existed toward us. I have seen the smile of disdain and the curl of the lip of scorn at the statement that one was a Mormon. During the thirty years of Senator Smoot's tenure of office, I have lived a great part of my time in the East in the same environment. . . . I want now to say to you, brethren and sisters, that, judged at any rate by my human wisdom and understanding, no other contributing cause equals that of the service which he has furnished, to the change that has come among the people of the earth who now honor and respect where formerly they scorned and despised. Furthermore Senator Smoot has given to his country a devoted service rarely equalled and never excelled."[2]

---

[1]*In Memory of Senator Reed Smoot*, Brigham Young University Library, 1966.
[2]*Conference Report*, April 1933, p. 102.

REED SMOOT

"A Few Words From Your Daughter Kirstine"

Together with Brother Widtsoe I had the privilege of visiting Europe during the months of July and August. While thus upon a special mission, and by the assistance of Brother Widtsoe, I had the privilege of visiting the Scandinavian countries. I also took the time during my last visit to go there, primarily, I will say, to visit my mother's old home. While a young man I used to say to mother: "Some day we will go back to the old home." I left it too late, as so many things are put off until it is too late; for my mother died when she was sixty years old. But I made up my mind that sooner or later I would go to the old home and see some of my relatives there. I haven't the time today to express to you the feelings I had when I stood upon the very spot where she was born, and when I saw the old door that she had opened perhaps hundreds and hundreds of times, when I looked upon the spring back of the house, that I had heard her speak of when I was a boy and, as I stood under the shade of that wonderful tree her mother had planted and which she used to tell me about; and as I saw conditions surrounding that homestead, I want to say to you, my brethren and sisters, I thanked God from the bottom of my heart that the gospel of Jesus Christ reached my mother, and that she knew it was true, when she was but a girl. All opposition and all persecution on the part of her father and her mother and her loved ones never had one iota of influence upon her testimony that God lived and that Jesus is the Christ.

My cousins brought to me the old family Bible, and as I lifted the lid I saw a writing and at the bottom of the last page of it the name "Anna Kirstine Maurits-datter." I could not read the writing, but I asked Brother Widtsoe to copy it as quickly as possible, then tell me what was in it. I desired to have it translated word for word. It was a message to her parents written on the day that she left home—the day she was driven from home by a loving father and mother who thought that she would not be gone very long, but that she would soon return and ask forgiveness, and deny that she knew that God lived and that Jesus is the Christ. She was only a girl, then, but I am going to take time now to read to this congregation, that letter, because it gives forth the spirit that makes women such as she. It is filled full of the spirit of our fathers and mothers who were willing to sacrifice all in this world for the gospel's sake; aye, it is the spirit of a missionary, teaching the gospel of Jesus Christ. This was written in her own hand writing, and it was the last farewell of a girl who loved her country, who loved her father and mother, and who loved her home, but who loved the gospel of Jesus Christ more:

A few words from your daughter Kirstine, Dear, my parents: Pray God for courage to accept this great truth contained in this book and now restored, so that rejected knowledge may not be a testimony against you on God's great day to come. I pray God that on that great day we may be able to gather together in joy and happiness, and that we may then be crowned to God's glory, and that he may say to us all: "Come now, my faithful children, you shall be rewarded for your labors." This matter, and my desire that you may know the truth and accept it, have made me shed in secret many burning tears, and they have been increased when I have thought of the ungodliness of mankind. The years are speeding on, the day is approaching when all must listen to the Shepherd and render obedience to his will, or receive punishment. The great King is coming to reign and to rule. Sin and evil will be banished. May God grant that you may be among the worthy ones. My heart grows tender when I think of these things. God give that all mankind may repent. I shall pray to my heavenly Father that all who read these lines may comprehend the true purpose of his holy book, and may lay down the burden of sin. That which I have written is for all who may read these lines. I pray God to lead you into eternal life.

Kirstine Maurits-datter, Drammen, Sept. 1, 1854.

I am not ashamed of the gospel of Jesus Christ; I am not ashamed of the testimony of the mother that gave me birth. I care not where I go upon the face of the earth, whether it be with kings, potentates, or any class of people in the world, I want them all to know that I am a member of the Church of Jesus Christ of Latter-day Saints. . . .

Conference Report, October 1923, pp. 76-77.

REED SMOOT

"Now That's a Big Lie"

When the Senator was a small boy, Brigham Young came to Provo and, at a conference meeting, said that the day would come when the human voice could be heard from New York to San Francisco. . . .

Reed's mother had taken him to this meeting, and on the way home he said (referring to what President Brigham Young had said), "Now that's a big lie. That's absolutely impossible. It couldn't be." His mother, who was a woman of very great faith, told her son, "Yes, you'll live to see the fulfillment of what the President has said today." He did not believe it. Time went by and while he was in the United States Senate, a broadcasting system was built so you could speak from New York City to San Francisco. One of his colleagues in the Senate had charge of this enterprise and when it was completed and they were to celebrate the event, he invited Senator Smoot to come to New York City and be the first man to speak over the completed network, which he did, and his voice was heard clearly and distinctly across the continent.

Thus he lived to literally fulfill the promise by President Brigham Young in Provo years before.

Hinckley, *Faith of Our Pioneer Fathers*, p. 207.

REED SMOOT

"Send Me Chances to Do a Little Good Each Day"

My mother taught me that the way to receive a testimony of this work, and the way to maintain it, is to never cease praying; and she promised me as my mother that if I would follow that course I should always have a knowledge that God lives, that Jesus is the Christ, and that this work is his work. Brethren and sisters, I have followed that counsel, and notwithstanding the positions to which I have been called that have taken me away from the body of the people, notwithstanding the year before that happened my avocation called me to meet men who actually ridiculed our belief and the question of God ever revealing himself to man, as being unreasonable and indefensible, thank God I have lived through it all. I thank God for the testimony I have that this is his work and that every prediction made by any servant of God in relation to it shall be fulfilled.

I pray God to "give me clean hands, clean words, and clean thoughts. Save me from habits that harm. Teach me to work as hard and play as fair in thy sight alone as if all the world saw. Forgive me when I am unkind, and help me to forgive those who are unkind to me. Keep me ready to serve others at some cost to myself. Send me chances to do a little good every day, and so grow more like Christ."

Conference Report, October 1931, p. 112.

———

REED SMOOT

"No One in This Audience Was More Astonished Than I"

My dear brethren and sisters, I feel exceedingly weak in standing before this vast audience this afternoon. No doubt many of you are surprised at my being called to this position, but I can assure you that no one in this audience was more astonished than I. Five years ago I was called by the mouthpiece of God to occupy a position in the presidency of the Utah Stake. That was a surprise to me at that time and I thought then that the Lord moves in a mysterious way. This afternoon when the mouthpiece of the Lord told me it was the will of the Lord that I should occupy a position as one of the Twelve Apostles, I certainly felt a more humble and more weak instrument in his hands for doing good than ever I did in my life. I beg of the brethren of the Twelve to bear with me in my mistakes. I beseech of you, my brethren and sisters, to give me your faith and prayers for I need them, and to fulfill this position that I am called to, I must have them. If I can be humble and have the confidence of the people and of the Priesthood, as God has called me so will I receive it in the same spirit; and as He gives me wisdom and light and revelation, just so far can I do His will and serve Him in this calling. If I did not know that Jesus was the Christ and that the Church of Jesus Christ of Latter-day Saints was His Church I can assure you that this calling that has been placed upon me would be the farthest from me to accept of any position that I could think of.

My life in the past has been in a business direction more than in any other way, and now that this change has come and this call from God has been placed upon me, I hope and trust that I will do nothing—aye, I would rather lose my right arm than to betray the confidence you have placed in me this day by voting for me in this position. My only desire is that God will give me power to perform the duties that shall devolve upon me acceptably in His sight, and acceptable to you, to the Apostles and to the mouthpiece of God upon this earth. To this end I beseech of you an interest in your faith and prayers that from now on I may be clothed with the Priesthood that will be some good to the children of men.

I ask God's choicest blessings upon His Church and upon every member thereof, that unity, peace and strength may be with us continually until we become a light unto the whole world, as has been predicted. In the name of Jesus Christ I ask it. Amen.

Conference Report, April 1900, pp. 52-53.

REED SMOOT

"I Would Be a Deacon"

In a conversation with Dr. [Creed] Haymond, James A. Farley, Postmaster General under President

Franklin Delano Roosevelt, said: "I am a Democrat of some national prominence, and Reed Smoot is a Republican; but I consider him to be the greatest diplomat in the United States Government. He knows more of what is going on, attends more meetings, and is a better authority on all that goes on than anyone else I know. I wish we had more men exactly like him.

"I have been reliably informed that Reed Smoot was offered the nomination for the Presidency of the United States, on the Republican ticket, if he would deny his faith—his being a Mormon would make it impossible for him to receive any such a nomination."

Dr. Haymond continued: "Fifteen years later, Senator Smoot was in my office and during the conversation, I told him what James Farley had told me. He said: 'In two national Republican Conventions, I was offered the nomination for President of the United States, if I could turn against my Church.'

"I said to him: 'Wouldn't it be worth it?'

"He whirled on me, took me by the arm and said: 'Young man, maybe you do not know my stand in regard to my Church. If I had to take my choice of being a deacon in the Church of Jesus Christ of Latter-day Saints, or being the President of the United States, I would be a deacon.' "

Hinckley, *The Faith of Our Pioneer Fathers*, pp. 201-202.

REED SMOOT

"Defend the Rights of the People"

The last time I visited Theodore Roosevelt he was a very, very sick man. It was some time before his death. In our conversation he expressed the opinion that the time was near at hand when he would be taken to the beyond. He said: "I have tried to live a Christian life, I believe in God, I have tried to wrong no man. I expect to continue my work beyond." He was strong enough to rise from his chair after a two hours' visit, and I had to leave to catch a train from New York to Washington. He arose with a great deal of energy, and putting his arm around me he said: "Reed, there are trying times coming for our country. I expect you to defend the rights of the people and the Constitution of the United States as long as you live." I promised him upon that occasion that I would do my best.

I love my country. I have watched her growth, I have seen her mistakes, as I judge them, but I have absolute confidence that there shall no harm come to our nation as a nation. We will revere the Constitution, live by its principles, even though at times it may seem that we are violating them. God bless America. God bless the Church of Jesus Christ of Latter-day Saints. God bless the Presidency of the Church, and give them the revelations, O Father, of thy mind and will, that they may at all times direct the affairs of this Church in a way that thou wilt approve of all that is done. And, O Father, grant unto thy servants power to defend thy cause here upon this earth in a way that will be convincing unto the honest in heart. May we grow in numbers as thou seest best we should, no faster, no slower, I pray in the name of Jesus Christ. Amen.

Conference Report, October 1935, p. 117.

—————

"This Night a Prayer Shall Go Up From My House"

I know as well as I know I live
that there is power in prayer. I do not know but what it would
be proper for me, at this time, to call attention to an experience
that I had four weeks ago today. Sunday afternoon I called at
the White House, to call upon the President. For days Mrs.
Harding had been lying at the point of death. The President
was in the sick room when I arrived, together with Dr. Mayhoe,
Dr. Finney, Dr. Harding and some three or four other prominent doctors. The attendant announced to the President that I
had called to see him, and he came out of the sick room into
his private office adjoining the sick room. He had been watching over Mrs. Harding for days and nights past, seeing each
day bring her nearer to the brink of the grave, and the doctors
had just decided that nothing would save her but an operation.
The question of the operation was left to the President for decision. The President said: "I have never had, in all my life,
a question brought to me for decision that I feel so helpless in
arriving at." I haven't the time to go into the details. Worried
as he was, haggard as he was, it seemed to me if any word of
encouragement could be given to him, it ought to have been
given. What a wonderful woman Mrs. Harding is, lying upon
her sick bed for days. When Dr. Finney was leaving the room,
she gave orders to take him down to the depot in the President's car, rather than send for one himself, and, while the
President and I were discussing questions affecting legislation,
on which he had asked me to make a report to him, and just
as I was about to leave, the attendant brought into the room a
beautiful box of roses, stating that Mrs. Harding had directed
him to bring them to me to Mrs. Smoot. Nobody thought that
Mrs. Harding would live through the night. The decision as
to an operation had to be reached, so the President told me,

before midnight; and, as I left the room, he came with me until we stood at the head of the stairs. I turned to the President and said, "President, there is hope yet. I have seen men and women raised from a death-bed. I know that there is power, Mr. President, in prayer—the wife can yet be saved. Do not be discouraged." And I said, "This night a prayer shall go up from my home, that God may spare her life, that she will not have to undergo an operation." He said to me: "Senator Smoot, I wish I knew that. I believe in prayer. I wish I knew that God through prayer would heal the sick." There were millions of people praying for her, from one end of the land to the other, but as those noted physicians sat around the bed, as midnight was approaching, there came a change. God had heard the prayers for her and the crisis had passed.

How many cases could we relate, testifying to just such power, and I hope and I trust that we will never forget that God rules the universe.

Conference Report, October 1922, p. 102-103.

REED SMOOT

"Reed, I Wish You Would Administer to Me"

Among the homes that I visited during my service in the Senate of the United States was the home of President Coolidge,[1] where I was invited several times. I never ate a mouthful of food at his home without a blessing upon it. Prayer was the practice of President Coolidge. The last time I visited him was shortly before his death. I sat by his bedside. We talked over conditions existing in our country, and when I was about to leave, the President said to me: "Senator, there is some plan in your Church, isn't there, where men administer to the sick and pray for them?" I said, "Yes, Mr. President. We call that administering to the sick." He said, "Can anyone in the Church administer to anyone outside of the Church?" I told him "Yes." He said, "Reed, I wish you would administer to me." I did so, and I want to say to you, my brothers and sisters, I never felt happier in my life than when I laid my hands upon him and asked God to bless him. He was a wonderful man, as nearly all of the American people knew him to be.

---

[1]Calvin Coolidge, President of the United States. *Conference Report*, April 1939, p. 56.

REED SMOOT

"Senator Smoot, Wasn't My Wine Good Enough for You?"

I would rather die than lose my testimony, and I have never been ashamed of it no matter where I have been. I have never occupied a position that man or woman could point to me and say, "He doesn't live up to the principles professed by him." In all of the gatherings of the men of the nation that I have attended, the great dinners given by the wealthy in Washington, where liquors were served at every banquet, never have I tasted a drop of their liquors or wines. At the first great banquet I attended, given by the wealthiest woman in the world, there were at every guest's place at the table glasses for the three different wines that were served. At the close of the dinner the hostess noticed that I had not taken a drop of these wines, and she said to me, "Senator Smoot, wasn't my wine good enough for you?"

I had a chance to explain to her the Word of Wisdom as understood by us. I begged of her to take no offense, for none was intended. It was not long until everyone in Washington— for I did the same at every dinner, at the embassies of foreign countries, or whatever the occasion might be—knew that I did not drink liquor. I thank God that I had strength enough to act as I professed, and as my religion taught me. . . . God never requires of his people anything that he does not provide a way for its accomplishment.

Conference Report, October 1935, p. 116.

REED SMOOT

"Family Devotion"

Do we teach our children to pray? If there is a home in all Zion; if there is a father or mother in the Church of Jesus Christ of Latter-day Saints, who do not teach their children to pray they will live to see the day when they will repent of that neglect.

I believe it was two years ago that Elder A. O. Woodruff in conference referred to the duty of praying in the family, not only praying but before prayers, reading some part of the scriptures, and advised all to do so. I accepted that advice.

We should designate a certain time, just before supper, or breakfast, or just after as the case may be, to get all the family together, and then take 10 or 15 minutes for the purpose of reading to them the word of God, and offering devotion to Him. I promise the father and mother who adopt this as a family rule that they will be blessed in so doing. Their children will bless them in years to come, and they will feel blessed in doing it as long as they live. I have heard others say they have adopted this plan for family devotion in their homes, and through it they have become better acquainted with the scriptures: that they have been better able to teach the Gospel of the Lord Jesus Christ than ever they were before. I earnestly ask every Latter-day Saint family to adopt this plan.

Conference Report, October 1903, p. 63.

REED SMOOT

"I Will Stop Next Time"

There is a saying that cleanliness is next to Godliness. . . .

I remember, when I was a small boy, President Brigham Young was making one his tours and arrived at a town in one of the southern counties. He had intended to stop there and speak to the people, but, as he drove along the streets, entering town, he noticed the unclean condition of the surroundings. He drove direct to the Bishop's home, stopped his team and said to the Bishop, who stood in front of his residence waiting the arrival of the president: "Why Bishop, I see the same old rocks upon the streets; I see the same old dirty surroundings; I see the same old gates off their hinges; I see the same old broken down fences; I see the same old puddles of mud before the tithing office and your public buildings, just as they were when I was last here; and, inasmuch as I called attention to these defects when I was here before, and it has had no effect upon the people whatever, I do not think it necessary for me to stop this time. Good-bye, Bishop. Tell the people when they attend to these things and rectify them, I will stop next time."

Conference Report, April 1903, p. 53.

Biographical Sketch

ELDER JAMES E. TALMAGE

Elder Talmage was born on September 21, 1862, at Hungerford, Berkshire, England, the son of James Joyce Talmage and his wife, Susannah Preater.

He was baptized and confirmed a member of The Church of Jesus Christ of Latter-day Saints at the place of his birth, June 15, 1873. The entire family left England May 24, 1876, landed in New York June 5 and arrived in Salt Lake City June 14.

On September 29, 1884, he was ordained a high priest, and was set apart as an alternate high counselor in the Utah Stake of Zion. On December 7, 1911, he was appointed to be one of the apostles, to fill the vacancy caused by the appointment of Elder Charles W. Penrose as second counselor in the First Presidency, and on the following day (December 8) he was ordained as an apostle of the Lord Jesus Christ and was set apart as one of the Council of the Twelve Apostles of The Church of Jesus Christ of Latter-day Saints, under the hands of President Joseph F. Smith, assisted by his counselors and members of the Council of the Twelve. On June 14, 1888, he married Mary May Booth at the Manti Temple, and from the union eight children were born.

In 1882-83 he took a selected course in chemistry and geology at Lehigh University, Bethlehem, Pennsylvania. He passed in his single year of residence nearly all the examinations in the four-year course and was later graduated; in 1883-84 he was engaged in advanced work at John Hopkins University, Baltimore, Maryland.

Elder Talmage was a brilliant scholar, teacher, lecturer and author. Two of his most famous books are *Jesus the Christ* and the *Articles of Faith.*

James Edward Talmage died July 27, 1933, at Salt Lake City.

JAMES E. TALMAGE

"Are We So Much Wiser Than the Bee?"

Sometimes I find myself under obligations of work requiring quiet and seclusion such as neither my comfortable office nor the cozy study at home insures. My favorite retreat is an upper room in the tower of a large building, well removed from the noise and confusion of the city streets. The room is somewhat difficult of access, and relatively secure against human intrusion. Therein I have spent many peaceful and busy hours with books and pen.

I am not always without visitors, however, especially in summertime; for, when I sit with windows open, flying insects occasionally find entrance and share the place with me. These self-invited guests are not unwelcome. Many a time I have laid down the pen and, forgetful of my theme, have watched with interest the activities of these winged visitants, with an afterthought that the time so spent had not been wasted, for, is it not true, that even a butterfly, a beetle, or a bee, may be a bearer of lessons to the receptive student?

A wild bee from the neighboring hills once flew into the room; and at intervals during an hour or more I caught the pleasing hum of its flight. The little creature realized that it was a prisoner, yet all its efforts to find the exit through the partly opened casement failed. When ready to close up the room and leave, I threw the window wide, and tried at first to guide and then to drive the bee to liberty and safety, knowing well that if left in the room it would die as other insects there entrapped had perished in the dry atmosphere of the enclosure. The more I tried to drive it out, the more determinedly did it oppose and resist my efforts. Its erstwhile peaceful hum developed into an angry roar, its darting flight became hostile and threatening.

Then it caught me off my guard and stung my hand—the hand that would have guided it to freedom. At last it alighted on a pendant attached to the ceiling, beyond my reach of help or injury. The sharp pain of its unkind sting aroused in me rather pity than anger. I knew the inevitable penalty of its mistaken opposition and defiance; and I had to leave the creature to its fate. Three days later I returned to the room and found the dried, lifeless body of the bee on the writing table. It had paid for its stubbornness with its life.

To the bee's short-sightedness and selfish misunderstanding I was a foe, a persistent persecutor, a mortal enemy bent on its destruction; while in truth I was its friend, offering it ransom of the life it had put in forfeit through its own error, striving to redeem it, in spite of itself, from the prison-house of death and restore it to the outer air of liberty.

Are we so much wiser than the bee that no analogy lies between its unwise course and our lives? We are prone to contend, sometimes with vehemence and anger, against the adversity which after all may be the manifestation of superior wisdom and loving care, directed against our temporary comfort for our permanent blessing. In the tribulations and sufferings of mortality there is a divine ministry which only the godless soul can wholly fail to discern. To many the loss of wealth has been a boon, a providential means of leading or driving them from the confines of selfish indulgence to the sunshine and the open, where boundless opportunity waits on effort. Disappointment, sorrow, and affliction may be the expression of an all-wise Father's kindness.

Consider the lesson of the unwise bee!

"Trust the Lord with all thine heart; and lean not unto thine own understanding.

"In all thy ways acknowledge him, and he shall direct thy paths." (Proverbs 3:5-6.)

The Improvement Era, November 1962, p. 817.

JAMES E. TALMAGE

"Look at the Engine Headlight"

During my college days, now more than a quarter of a century past, I was one of a class of students appointed to fieldwork as a part of our prescribed courses in geology,—the science that deals with the earth in all of its varied aspects and phases, but more particularly with its component rocks, the structural features they present, the changes they have undergone and are undergoing—the science of worlds.

A certain assignment had kept us in the field many days. We had traversed, examined, and charted, miles of lowlands and uplands, valleys and hills, mountain heights and canyon defiles. As the time allotted to the investigation drew near its close, we were overtaken by a violent windstorm, followed by a heavy snow,—unseasonable and unexpected, but which, nevertheless, increased in intensity so that we were in danger of being snowbound in the hills. The storm reached its height while we were descending a long and steep mountain-side several miles from the little railway station, at which we had hoped to take the train that night for home. With great effort we reached the station late at night, while the storm was yet raging. We were suffering from the intense discomfiture, we learned that the expected train had been stopped by snow-drifts a few miles from the little station at which we waited.

The station was but an isolated telegraph-post: the station-house comprised but one small room, a mile away from the nearest village. The reason for the maintenance of a telegraph-post at this point was found in the dangerous nature of the road in the vicinity, and the convenient establishment of a water-tank to supply the engines. The train for which we so expectantly and hopefully waited, was the Owl Express—a fast night train connecting large cities. Its time-schedule permitted stops at but few and these the most important stations; but, as we knew, it had to stop at this out-of-the-way post, to replenish the water supply of the locomotive.

Long after midnight the train arrived, in a terrific whirl of wind and snow. I lingered behind my companions, as they hurriedly clambered aboard, for I was attracted by the engineer, who, during the brief stop, while his assistant was attending to the water replenishment, bustled about the engine, oiling some parts, adjusting others, and generally overhauling the panting locomotive. I ventured to speak to him, busy though he was. I asked how he felt on such a night,—wild, weird, and furious, when the powers of destruction seemed to be let loose, abroad and uncontrolled, when the storm was howling and when danger threatened from every side. I thought of the possibility—the probability even—of snow-drifts or slides on the track; of bridges and high trestles, which may have been loosened by the storm; of rock-masses dislodged from the mountain-side;—of these and other possible obstacles. I realized that in the event of accident through obstruction on or disruption of the track, the engineer and the fireman would be the ones most exposed to danger; a violent collision would most likely cost them their lives. All of these thoughts and others I expressed in hasty questioning of the bustling, impatient engineer.

His answer was a lesson not yet forgotten. In effect he said, though in jerky and disjointed sentences: "Look at the engine headlight. Doesn't that light up the track for a hundred yards or more? Well, all I try to do is to cover that hundred yards of lighted track. That I can see, and for that distance I know the road-bed is open and safe. And," he added, with what, through the swirl and the dim lamp-lighted darkness of the roaring night, I saw was a humorous smile on his lips, and a merry twinkle of his eye, "believe me, I have never been able to drive this old engine of mine, God bless her! so fast as to outstrip that hundred yards of lighted track. The light of the engine is always ahead of me!"

As he climbed to his place in the cab, I hastened to board the first passenger coach; and, as I sank into the cushioned seat, in blissful enjoyment of the warmth and general comfort, offering strong contrast to the wildness of the night without, I thought deeply of the words of the grimy, oil-stained engineer. They were full of faith—the faith that accomplishes great things, the faith that gives courage and determination, the faith that leads to works. What if the engineer had failed; had yielded to fright and fear; had refused to go on because of the threatening dangers? Who knows what work may have been hindered; what great plans may have been nullified; what God-appointed commissions of mercy and relief may have been thwarted, had the engineer weakened and quailed?

For a little distance the storm-swept track was lighted up for that short space the engineer drove on!

We may not know what lies ahead of us in the future years nor even in the days or hours immediately beyond. But for a few yards, or possibly only a few feet, the track is clear, our duty is plain, our course is illumined. For that short distance for the next step, lighted by the inspiration of God, go on!

The Improvement Era, July 1914, pp. 807-809.

Biographical Sketch

Elder Whitney was born to Horace Kimball Whitney and Helen Mar Kimball on July 1, 1855, in Salt Lake City, Utah.

He was educated in the schools of Salt Lake and the University of Deseret. Later he became Chancellor of the University of Utah.

He filled three missions for the Church, the last of which he presided over the European Mission.

For twenty-eight years Elder Whitney served as bishop of the Eighteenth Ward of Salt Lake City, after which he was called to the Council of the Twelve Apostles.

He was ordained an apostle April 9, 1906, by Joseph F. Smith. He was fifty years old when he became a member of the Quorum of the Twelve. Elder Whitney taught in the Brigham Young College in Logan, Utah, and published two biographies, one on Heber C. Kimball and the other on Lorenzo Snow.

Outstanding among his literary works is a history of Utah. He was a most effective speaker and famed as a writer. Elder Whitney could hold an audience spellbound by reading his own poems. In his youth he was much interested in dramatics and took prominent parts in the "Home Dramatic Company" productions. He also sang and was active in political circles.

He died of a heart attack May 16, 1931, at Salt Lake City, Utah.

ORSON F. WHITNEY

"Judge Not the Lord by Feeble Sense"

Love of God, the very essence of religion, was always with me. I never doubted the Lord's existence, his goodness or his power. When in trouble my first thought was to pray to Him. I did not share the notion, expressed by some of my fellows, that "the Lord doesn't want us to bother him about every little thing." I have never believed that we trouble our Heavenly Father by craving blessings at his hand. Prayer is an expression of faith, and the exercise of faith, whereby comes spiritual development, is one of the great objects and privileges of this earthly existence, our "second estate," where we "walk by faith," as before we "walked by sight." I believed then and believe now, that God's ear is as open to the pleadings of a little child, as to the prayers of a congregation. . . .

A rather remarkable experience befell me when a child. I had lost my pocket knife—the first I ever owned. Grieving bitterly over the misfortune, I almost questioned Providence for permitting it to happen. Yes, I was just that unreasonable, not knowing any better, and being so constituted that it nearly tore my heart out to lose anything upon which I had set my affections. While sorrowing over my loss, I suddenly felt an influence of peace, and as I looked up to heaven through my tears, a ray of light seemed resting down upon me. All at once those splendid lines of Cowper's flashed into my mind:

> Judge not the Lord by feeble sense,
>   But trust Him for His grace;
> Behind a frowning Providence
>   He hides a smiling face.

Never to my knowledge had I seen or heard that verse before. But be that as it may, it had the effect of drying my tears and giving me the assurance that I should find my lost knife. A few minutes later I walked down the path to my mother's gate, and there, half hidden in the dust, lay my precious treasure. How eagerly I pounced upon it, and how grateful I was for its recovery, I need not say.

To some this incident may appear trivial. To me, it is anything but that.

Orson F. Whitney, *Through Memory's Halls* (Independence: Press of Zion's Printing and Publishing Company, 1930), pp. 70-71.

ORSON F. WHITNEY

"That Will Depend Entirely Upon Yourself"

Then came a marvelous manifestation, and admonition from a higher source, one impossible to ignore. It was a dream, or a vision in a dream, as I lay upon my bed in the little town of Columbia, Lancaster County, Pennsylvania. I seemed to be in the Garden of Gethsemane, a witness of the Savior's agony. I saw Him as plainly as I have seen anyone. Standing behind a tree in the foreground, I beheld Jesus, with

Peter, James and John, as they came through a little wicket gate at my right. Leaving the three Apostles there, after telling them to kneel and pray, the Son of God passed over to the other side, where He also knelt and prayed. It was the same prayer with which all Bible readers are familiar: "Oh my Father, if it be possible, let this cup pass from me; nevertheless not as I will but as Thou wilt."

As He prayed the tears streamed down His face, which was towards me. I was so moved at the sight that I also wept, out of pure sympathy. My whole heart went out to Him; I loved Him with all my soul, and longed to be with Him as I longed for nothing else.

Presently He arose and walked to where those Apostles were kneeling—fast asleep! He shook them gently, awoke them, and in a tone of tender reproach, untinctured by the least show of anger or impatience, asked them plaintively if they could not watch with Him one hour. There He was, with the awful weight of the world's sin upon His shoulders, with the pangs of every man, woman and child shooting through His sensitive soul—and they could not watch with Him one poor hour!

Returning to His place, He offered up the same prayer as before; then went back and again found them sleeping. Again He awoke them, readmonished them, and once more returned and prayed. Three times this occurred, until I was perfectly familiar with His appearance—face, form and movements. He was of noble stature and majestic mien—not at all the weak, effeminate being that some painters have portrayed; but the very God that He was and is, as meek and humble as a little child.

All at once the circumstance seemed to change, the scene remaining just the same. Instead of before, it was after the crucifixion, and the Savior, with the three Apostles now stood together in a group at my left. They were about to depart and ascend to Heaven. I could endure it no longer. I ran from behind the tree, fell at His feet, clasped Him around the knees, and begged Him to take me with Him.

I shall never forget the kind and gentle manner in which He stooped, raised me up, and embraced me. It was so vivid, so real. I felt the very warmth of His body, as He held me in His arms and said in tenderest tones: "No my son; these have finished their work; they can go with me; but you must stay and finish yours." Still I clung to Him. Gazing up into His face—for He was taller than I—I besought Him fervently: "Well, promise me that I will come to you at the last." Smiling sweetly, He said: "That will depend entirely upon yourself." I awoke with a sob in my throat, and it was morning.

"That's from God," said Elder Musser, when I related to him what I had seen and heard. "I do not need to be told that," was my reply. I saw the moral clearly. I have never thought of being an Apostle, nor of holding any other office in the Church, and it did not occur to me then. Yet I knew that these sleeping Apostles meant me. I was asleep at my post—as any man is who, having been divinely appointed to do one thing, does another.

But from that hour, all was changed. I never was the same man again.

Whitney, *Through Memory's Halls*, pp. 82-83.

ORSON F. WHITNEY

"I Answered, I Do Pray"

One morning I was endeavoring to write the usual editorial, but could make no headway, and wore out the whole day in a vain attempt to produce something worth reading. At last I threw down my pen and burst into tears of vexation.

Just then the Good Spirit whispered: "Why don't you pray?"

As if a voice had addressed me audibly, I answered, "I do pray." I was praying five times a day—secret prayers, morning, noon and night; and vocal prayers, with the rest of the household, at a breakfast and dinner time. "I do pray—why can't I get some help," I asked almost petulantly, for I was heartsick and half discouraged.

"Pray now," said the Spirit, "and ask for what you want."

I saw the point. It was a special not a general prayer that was needed. I knelt and sobbed out a few simple words. I did not pray for the return of the Ten Tribes nor for the building of the New Jerusalem. I asked the Lord in the name of Jesus Christ to help me write that article. I then arose, seated myself, and began to write. My mind was now perfectly clear, and my pen fairly flew over the paper. All I needed came as fast as I could set it down—every thought, every word in place. In a short time the article was completed to my entire satisfaction. I read it to the President, and he approved it without the change of a syllable.

This taught me a lesson; or rather, it reminded me of one I already knew, but needed to have emphasized. Prayer is not a matter of mere words, not a string of stereotyped phrases. It is "the soul's sincere desire," and it was of such a prayer, and no other, that the Lord said: "Ask, and ye shall receive."

Whitney, *Through Memory's Halls*, pp. 151-52.

ORSON F. WHITNEY

"The Pain Has Gone"

It was April 8, 1877, when I left Columbia for Elyria, Ohio. Arriving at my destination, I walked three miles into the country, to the farm where dwelt the Frinks. They were not aware of my coming, but had been praying that an Elder of the Church might be led that way, several of their neighbors, with whom Sister Frink had conversed, having expressed a desire to hear more of the Gospel, and hear it from the lips of a 'Mormon' missionary. I was the only one in that part of the country.

On the other side of the country road passing the farm house where I was staying, stood the residence of Truman Frink's brother, a bitter anti-Mormon, who had been heard to say that if one of our Elders crossed his threshold he would kick him into the street. . . . His wife, Margaret Frink, was an excellent woman, childless by him but by a former husband the mother of several daughters, all married. The eldest, a widow with one child, shared her mother's home.

Mrs. Frink had been confined to her room with an attack of neuralgia, which for many weeks had caused her intense pain. Her daughter had learned . . . that . . . healing was practiced by the Latter-day Saints. . . . She therefore invited me to come and bless her mother, that she might be healed. Sister 'Angie' seconded the suggestion—if, indeed, she did not originate it—and again I was all but paralyzed at the prospect.

Never did I feel so helpless—or so humble. I besought the the Lord with all my soul to stand by me in this critical hour, to perfect my faith, and use me, if He could consistently, as an instrument for showing forth His merciful power upon the afflicted one. I then consecrated, as best I could, some olive oil provided by Sister Frink, and went with her and her husband to Mrs. Frink's abode.

It was evening and the family were all at home. The daughter met us at the door, and ushered us into her mother's apartment, on the right of a hallway leading through the house, with rooms on either side. We had heard, as we entered, men's gruff voices and loud laughter in a room to the left; and presently Eli Frink thrust his head through a rear doorway, glanced around suspiciously, and then retired without uttering a word.

Mrs. Frink, with her head bandaged, was sitting up, but still suffering much pain. Laying my hands upon her head, which

I previously had anointed, I proceeded to bless her. Scarcely had I begun, when a power fell upon me that I had never felt before. . . . It was a warm glow in my throat and breast—not painful, but powerful, almost preventing utterance, and it ran like liquid flame to the very tips of my fingers. The effect was instant. "Thank God!" said the sufferer, "the pain has gone." . . . I was so overcome by a sense of gratitude for this signal manifestation of divine favor, that I sank into a chair and burst into tears.

Whitney, *Through Memory's Halls*, pp. 85-87.

ORSON F. WHITNEY

"The Best Bishop in the Church"

My installation as Bishop came about in this manner. On my way to church that Sabbath evening I pursued an indirect course, lengthening my walk from the parental home on City Creek to the Deseret Bank corner, where, as I turned to go east, I was accosted by Laron Cummings, who had a room on an upper floor of the Bank building.

"Come up to my room," said Laron.

"Thank you," said I, "but I must go to meeting. They are going to put me in Bishop tonight."

He laughed, and I laughed and passed on, little dreaming that I had uttered in jest a prediction that was about to be fulfilled. I had been told that a new Bishopric could be installed that night, but as to the proposed personnel I knew nothing.

When the President of the Stake said to the congregation:

"It has been moved and seconded that Orson F. Whitney be the Bishop of the Eighteenth Ward," I was astounded. If the earth had opened and swallowed me, I could scarcely have been more surprised. An unmarried youth, just turned twenty-three, with scarcely any experience in Church work, to preside over a ward where Youngs, Kimballs, Caines, Calders and other noted families dwelt!—the thought was overpowering; it almost took my breath.

Called upon to express my feelings, I tremblingly took the stand and tremulously addressed the large congregation. I told them—what they already knew—that I was young and inexperienced; but that time would cure those defects; and I accepted my call to the bishopric as I had accepted my call to the mission field, trusting in the Lord to qualify me for my duties.

President Daniel H. Wells, for many years one of the First Presidency, but since President Young's death a Counselor to the Twelve Apostles; George Q. Cannon, Joseph F. Smith and Brigham Young, Jr., all members of that quorum; with the Stake Presidency, Angus M. Cannon, Joseph E. Taylor and David O. Calder, then laid their hands upon my head, and President Wells ordained me a High Priest and set me apart to preside over the Eighteenth Ward as its Bishop.

George Q. Cannon then addressed the meeting. "Bishop Whitney," he remarked, "said a good thing when he told us that time would remedy in him the defects of youth and inexperience. And I will add this: If the people of this ward will rally round him and hold up his hands, the time will come when they will think they have the best bishop in the Church."

He did not say that I would be the best bishop—and of course I never was; but he said the people would think so; and that prophecy was abundantly fulfilled. During the well-nigh twenty-eight years of my bishopric, I had the love and loyal support of the good people of the Eighteenth Ward. They thought me the best bishop, just as children in a family think their father the best of men. It does not have to be fact. It is a sentiment, and a wholesome one, an expression of loyalty akin to patriotism, the love of one's own native land.

The President of the Stake followed with a jocular allusion

to my unmarried status, quoting Paul the Apostle on "blameless" bishops and matrimony, and adding: "We are pleased to hear Brother Whitney say that he will endeavor to qualify himself." Thus the incident closed.

Whitney, *Through Memory's Halls*, pp. 106-107.

ORSON F. WHITNEY

"He Did Not Say Which Child It Was"

Meanwhile another stroke of affliction had fallen upon me and mine. The day that witnessed the beginning of that first memorable jaunt into the country bordering on London, my infant son, Heber Kimball Whitney, died at the home of his Grandfather Smoot, in far-off Utah. This child was born seven months and twenty-one days after I left for England. Consequently I had not seen him, and would not now behold him in this world.

The sad word reached me in a letter of condolence from President John Henry Smith at Liverpool; he having read it in the Deseret News. Later it was confirmed by a message from my father-in-law at Provo. It was all the more woeful because of the painful circumstances connected with it—my wife's illness, her mother's death, and the crushing out of the fond hope that the coming of this little one would prove a lasting solace to her wounded spirit.

Controlling my feelings as best I could, I penned an epistle of love and sympathy to my heart-broken wife. It closed thus:

"I am very anxious to hear from you, Darling, and yet

fear to receive the next message, lest it bring more bad news. May God comfort you, for surely you need comfort now.

"President Smith was the first to inform me. But as he did not say which child it was, I was left in suspense for some hours, though all the while feeling sure that it must be the baby, having received from you the news of his critical illness.

"The President has offered to release me. He says I may go with his blessing. I suppose I ought to accept the offer, for he is the Lord's representative in these lands. How do you feel about it? It is too late to sail with the May company, but I could start in June. If you say so, and the Lord does not direct otherwise, I will come."

Whitney, *Through Memory's Halls*, pp. 166-67.

ORSON F. WHITNEY

"In a Lake of Living Fire"

Among my newly formed acquaintances in Cleveland was a very estimable lady, the widow of a Union officer who had fallen in battle during the Civil War. She loved her departed husband, tenderly cherished his memory, and frequently expressed for him the fondest and deepest devotion. When I explained to her the doctrines of salvation for the dead and marriage for eternity, stating that these were among the purposes for which Latter-day Saints build Temples and officiate therein, she was greatly interested, and put to me this pointed question:

"Do you mean to tell me that if I become a Latter-day

Saint I can have such work done for my dear husband, and be his wife in another world?"

"Yes," I answered.

Then this from her: "I have never heard anything so beautiful, so sublime. Convince me of it, and I will be baptized, though it were in a lake of living fire."

To which I replied: "I cannot convince you, but the Lord can and will if you ask Him."

She said she would; and no doubt she did, for not long afterwards I received a note from her, stating that she had received the testimony she sought, and was ready to be baptized.

Immediately I wrote, telling her that I would make up a little party and meet her at a given time and place on the shore of Lake Erie, and there baptize her. The party was made up and about ready to start, when there came another note from her, reading as follows: "I never knew till now what a poor, weak, frail creature I am. I thought myself brave enough to take this step; but I am not. If I should become a 'Mormon' all my friends would forsake me, I would lose my social standing, and my name would be cast out as evil. I cannot make the sacrifice. And yet I believe the doctrine true, and that you are a real servant of God. I hope the time will come when we can stand upon the same plane and be brother and sister in the Church of Christ; but I cannot do that now."

It was with mixed feelings of sorrow and pity that I perused this communication. How like the impetuous Apostle, I thought—he who said to the Master: "Though I should die with thee, yet will I not deny thee." But he thrice denied that he knew the Holy One by whom he had vowed to stand. And this good woman—for she was a good woman, a child of Israel, no doubt, else why did she believe?—supposed herself willing to be baptized "in a lake of living fire." But when the test came she was found wanting. Let us hope that like the penitent Peter, who so nobly redeemed himself, she may yet turn and make amends. . . .

Whitney, *Through Memory's Halls*, pp. 96-97.

Biographical Sketch

ELDER JOHN A. WIDTSOE

John A. Widtsoe was born on January 31, 1872, at Daloe, Island of Froyen, Trondhjem, Norway, the son of John A. Widtsoe and Anna Karine Gaarden.

Elder Widtsoe immigrated with his mother and brother (his father was deceased) to the United States. As a child and young man he lived in Logan, Utah, and received his early education there.

He was a brilliant student and later attended Harvard, where he graduated summa cum laude. By showing excellent and wide acquaintance in one line of study or for uniform excellence in all subjects taken, young John Widtsoe won in both.

When he was graduated from Harvard, four widely varying positions were open to him. He could have remained as a teacher at Harvard, or become a research chemist for a great national and international industrial enterprise or he could have joined the editorial staff of an important magazine. Lastly he could go back to the Agricultural College at Logan as a teacher of chemistry. He resolved the conflict upon the basis of his conclusion that his state needed most his services as a scientist. Elder Widtsoe gained world renown in his academic field.

At the time he was called to the Quorum of Twelve, March 17, 1921, he was President of the University of Utah.

Elder John Andreas Widtsoe died November 29, 1952, at Salt Lake City.

In the concluding paragraph of *In a Sunlit Land*, the story of his life, he wrote: "I hope it will be said of me I have tried to live unselfishly, to serve God and help my fellow men, and use my time and talents industriously for the advancement of human good."

That desire has been fulfilled.

JOHN A. WIDTSOE

"A Mormon Tract Was Stuffed Into Each Shoe"

One day she [John A. Widtsoe's mother] asked a neighbor, a ship's captain living in the same house, an older resident, to recommend a shoemaker to whom she might take her son's shoes for repair. One Olaus Johnsen, a very competent, honest workman was recommended. In fact, the shoemaker's son Arnt brought to the house a pair of the captain's shoes, and took with him for repair, a pair of John's shoes. When the boy's shoes were returned, a Mormon tract was stuffed into each shoe. A little later, with a parcel containing another pair of old shoes, the widow set forth in the warm sunshine of the spring of 1879 for the half-hour walk to Johnsen's shoemaker shop. It certainly did not occur to her that she was making the most fateful visit of her life. Yet, who can say that it was the most fateful. The events of life are like the threads of a tapestry—all together make the pattern and picture.

Olaus Johnsen was a wholesome, well-spoken man in his forties, a workman who knew his craft. His wife was of the sturdy Norwegian type. Anna Widtsoe first met the wife, and made inquiry about the meaning of the tracts found in her son's shoes that had been returned, repaired. Mrs. Johnsen declared that they told the truth, but that Mr. Johnsen would explain the whole matter.

The shoemaker agreed to put soles on the shoes, strong enough to last a good while even under the wear of a lively, active lad, who was always moving about. The details of the business were soon agreed upon; the commonplaces of courteous people were exchanged; the widow was about to leave the shop, yet a little curious about the tracts which she had found in the first pair of shoes when they were returned, but unwilling to ask too many questions.

Anna Widtsoe's hand was on the door latch, when the shoemaker said, somewhat hesitatingly, for the business was concluded and the lady was a stranger, "You may be surprised to hear me say that I can give you something of more value than soles for your child's shoes." She was surprised. She looked into the eyes of the man, who stood straight and courageous in his shop.

"What can you, a shoemaker, give me better than soles for my son's shoes? You speak in riddles," she answered.

The shoemaker did not hesitate. "If you will but listen, I can teach you the Lord's true plan of salvation for His children. I can teach you how to find happiness in this life, and to prepare for eternal joy in the life to come. I can tell you whence you came, why you are upon earth, and where you will go after death. I can teach you, as you have never known it before, the love of God for His children on earth."

Understanding, happiness, joy, love—the words with which she was wrestling! But, this was a shoemaker shop. This man was clearly a humble man who knew little of the wisdom of schools and churches. She felt confused. She simply asked, "Who are you?"

"I am a member of the Church of Christ—we are called Mormons. We have the truth of God."

Mormons! It was terrible. She had innocently walked into a dangerous place. Hurriedly she thanked the shoemaker, left the shop, and climbed the hill.

Yet, as she walked homeward, the words of the shoemaker rang in her ears; and she remembered a certain power in his voice and majesty in his bearing when he delivered his message and bore his testimony. He was a shoemaker, but no ordinary man. Could it really be that the Mormons had the truth of the Lord? No, it was absurd! But, it made her thoughtful and restless. When the repaired shoes were brought to the house a day or two later, by the shoemaker's young son, Arnt Johnsen, Anna Widtsoe found, carefully tucked into each shoe, other Mormon tracts. The shoemaker was valiant. He missed no opportunity to fulfill the obligation of a Latter-day Saint, to bear witness modestly and properly but steadily, to all the world.

Then began two years of struggle.

The tracts in the shoes aroused her curiosity to the extent that one Sunday she went to a Mormon meeting. The meeting room was on the second floor of the shoemaker's home, a sturdy log house. A small group of people were there; and a fiery speaker, a missionary, raised all manner of questions in her mind. The main effect of that meeting was a resentment against the primitive environment of the meeting. Very humble people constituted the membership of the Trondhjem Branch. Foolish class distinctions were sharply drawn in the land. Anna Widtsoe, though a fishermaiden, had been well born, in the economic as well as in the moral sense; and she had moved upward with the years. She was now of the professional class. To join such a group as she saw there that Sunday seemed to her tradition-bound mind to be a step downward. Had she understood the gospel, such distinctions would have been meaningless. One day, some months later, when the truth was forcing itself upon her, she came home, stood quietly in the middle of the floor, and said aloud, to herself, "Must I step down to that? Yes, if it is the truth, I must do so."

Soon, however, all else was forgotten in her battles with the shoemaker and the missionaries upon points of doctrine. She knew her Bible. Time upon time she came prepared to vanquish the elders, only to meet defeat herself. She had not read the Bible as these men did. Gradually she began to comprehend that her reading had been colored and overshadowed by the teachings of the church of her childhood; and that these men, these Mormon missionaries, accepted the Bible in a truer, more literal manner. She liked it. Nevertheless, she fought fearlessly. It was no use. At length she had to admit that the Bible was all on the side of the Mormons.

Even then she was not ready. There were other matters to be settled. Questions of authority, revelation, life within the Church, and a hundred others that her quick mind formulated, were presented to the missionaries, debated, discussed and taken up again. She had a worthy teacher in the missionary then in Trondhjem, Elder Anthon L. Skanchy, whose knowledge of the gospel was extensive and sound, and whose wisdom in leading inquirers to truth was unusually fine. This well-informed, intelligent widow tested his powers. Upon her he directed the full battery of gospel evidence. Unwillingly, yet prayerfully, she became convinced that she was in the presence of eternal truth.

At length, on April 1, 1881, a little more than two years after she first heard the gospel, she was baptized into the Church by Elder Anthon L. Skanchy. Thin ice still lay over the edges of the fjord, which had to be broken to permit the ordinance to be performed. The water was icy cold. Yet, she declared to her dying day that never before in all her life had she felt warmer or more comfortable than when she came out of the baptismal waters of old Trondhjem's fjord. The fire within was kindled, never to be extinguished. The humble people of the branch became her brethren and sisters. She loved them and rejoiced in their company.

John A. Widtsoe, *In the Gospel Net* (Salt Lake City: Bookcraft, 1966), pp. 53-57.

"The Sound of the Daily Mail Cart"

Two months before we were to sail from Oslo,[1] I was sent to my father's oldest sister who with her husband lived in the country some twenty-five miles north of Oslo. There I spent happy weeks among the fields and forests on the two large estates that my uncle was managing.

My aunt was scandalized that any member of the family had become besmirched with Mormonism. She was determined to prevent the oldest son of her beloved brother from going to Utah. . . . Therefore, she arranged that a few days before my mother's expected arrival, I was to be sent into the mountain districts, so far away that I could not brought back in time for the sailing of the boat. And should the stubborn mother miss the boat to recover her son, no one would know where her son was. It was a perfect plan, which, of course, was unknown to me. I understood only that I was going into the mountains for an outing.

The day for my departure came. My belongings were all packed. The horses were at the door. We were at breakfast. Suddenly there was the sound of the daily mail cart, which also carried passengers. It stopped in front of the house. Out stepped my mother with my brother Osborne, just one week earlier than the set date! My aunt's consternation was inexpressible. Even now I must smile at the episode. Yet, even then, my aunt wanted to take me into the mountains, "for a change." She also was of the stern kind. But my mother was unyielding. "We leave for Oslo this afternoon." Thus, I was not kidnapped, and another "best-laid" plan was foiled. Why my mother left her home a week early she could not explain. "I just had to leave then." So the Lord guides his faithful children.

[1]For America and Utah.
John A. Widtsoe, *In a Sunlit Land* (Salt Lake City: Deseret News Press, 1952), pp. 7-8.

"The Luxury of That Coal"

On Saturday, November 15, 1883, Anna Gaarden Widtsoe and her two sons landed in Logan, Utah, their destination. . . .

The first two or three days were spent under the hospitable roof of Bishop Anthon L. Skanchy and his family; after which she moved into a one-room house in a large yard, on the southern edge of the city. Bishop Skanchy who had brought her into the Church helped her secure the necessary furniture for meagre but comfortable living. The widow and her children playfully laid off the floor of their one room into four parts, living room, dining room, bedroom and kitchen. Blessed with the power of imagination, the little family soon saw the tiny house as a mansion. New life began happily, though the little money remaining was fast melting away. . . .

Actual want there was not. The organization of the Church provided against suffering, should it occur, and kindly friends and neighbors were anxious to give the newcomers a helping hand. One evening during the first, bitter cold winter in Logan, the widow put her last stick of wood into the stove. Then she called her two boys to her side. Together they kneeled down and told the Lord of their condition, and asked him for fuel so that they might keep warm. Within five minutes after their prayer was over, there was a knock on the door, and Brother Larsen living some distance up the street, and barely an acquaintance, came in with a big sack of coal upon his back, for the emigrant family. The prayer had been answered, almost before it was uttered. The luxury of that coal, the first they had in Zion, and the knowledge that the Lord was near, made the evening one of rare joy.

Widtsoe, *In the Gospel Net* (Bookcraft), pp. 65-67.

"Sister Widtsoe Is Not a Beggar, Yet"

It was pride, foolish pride, perhaps, rather than necessity, that on several occasions led the little family in those early days to the brink of want. In the spring of 1884 Anna Widtsoe moved into a two room house—a noble rise in fortune—nearer the business centre and in another ward so that her customers would not have so far to go. Collections were slow one month; John was out of work. At last the family had only a sack of "shorts" left. For three weeks, they lived on "shorts" and water. Never before, in man's history, had "shorts" been served in so many different dishes as the widow's ingenuity devised. Nevertheless, the diet was frightfully monotonous. They did not know, then, the high nutritive value of "shorts." One day, after nearly three weeks of rations on "shorts" and water, the sixth ward had a ward reunion. A Mormon ward reunion includes a feast of all the good things of earth, or nearly all. When the meal was ended, there was food left over, and the good-hearted Bishop Skanchy—and no man was ever kinder to the poor—filled a large basket with roast chicken and lamb, vegetables and bread, cakes and desserts, and sent them by a messenger to the widow and her sons, who now lived in the first ward. When the "shorts"-filled boys saw the well filled basket of goodies uncovered upon their table, there was eager, anticipating swallowing, and much inward joy; all of which was changed to darkest despair when the widow drew herself up to her full height and said, "Brother, please take the basket back to the bishop with my thanks, and say to him that Sister Widtsoe is not a beggar, yet." To the boys, the departure of that basket with its contents, was the darkest moment of their first years in Zion. It seemed a foolish pride, but perhaps it was better for the family to nurse a stubborn independence.

Widtsoe, *In the Gospel Net* (Bookcraft), pp. 67-68.

"Get Behind Me, Satan"

She [Anna Widtsoe] had not been taught the Word of Wisdom, except as it had been mentioned casually in her Gospel conversations. Now, she began to understand its real meaning and purpose and the necessity of obeying it as it was the desire of the Father that his children should heed it. Like nearly all of her country people she had drunk coffee from her childhood, and was an occasional user of tea. Alcoholic beverages she did not use. She set about to give up the use of tea and coffee, but found it difficult. When she sewed every night far beyond midnight, the cup of coffee seemed to freshen her, she thought. After a two months' struggle she came home one day, having given serious consideration to the Word of Wisdom problem. Her mind was made up. She stood in the middle of the room and said aloud, "Never again. Get behind me, Satan!" and walked briskly to her cupboard, took out the packages of coffee and tea and threw them on the fire. From that day she never used tea or coffee.

Widtsoe, *In the Gospel Net* (Bookcraft), p. 73.

"The Lord Had Given the Boys to Her"

Her house was not yet built when she decided that John must no longer be kept from regular schooling. He was well employed and giving satisfaction; soon he would be able to provide for the family. To take him out of such employment, to get a bit more book learning, considering that they were a family of poor immigrants, seemed very unwise to many good people. The bishop remonstrated with the widow. "The boy would become lazy. He should be in the canyon now, learning to do hard work. His boys were trained to work. She should be content with what she had." The widow listened politely, though the storm was gathering. She was never afraid to speak her mind when occasion arose. "She was grateful for the bishop's interest; he meant well. But, the Lord had given the boys to her and not to the bishop. They were her responsibility, not his. She had obligations to the living and the dead which he did not know about. Besides, he did not understand, as she did, that the training of the mind is as necessary as the training of the muscles. She concluded by looking into the future, and predicting that he and others would yet admit that she was right; and that the time would come when all children would be given the opportunity of higher education." The good man, for he was a kind, generous man, limited in his vision by his own hard pioneer experience, saw that nothing could be done to change the widow's mind, and that the boy would have to go on to possible destruction!

Widtsoe, *In the Gospel Net* (Bookcraft), pp. 78-79.

"With Eyes Now Blazing"

During this time, as always, she was firm in her devotion to the Gospel. The eternal truth restored through the Prophet Joseph Smith was the joy of her life. That faith she knew must be kept untarnished. That must be defended at all costs. She was everywhere the upholder of the Church, its principles and officers. At times this attitude was put to the test. For example, about 1896, Moses Thatcher, an apostle of the Church, was suspended from service in the Quorum of Twelve Apostles. Brother Thatcher, a man of unusual gifts and most charming personality, was very popular in his home town of Logan, as throughout the Church. His suspension caused wide-spread discussion, and many of his intimate Logan friends felt that he had been treated unjustly, and took his side against the action of the authorities of the Church. The temporary unheaval was tempestuous. Men's feelings ran high. While the excitement was at its height, two of the ward elders called at the Widtsoe home as ward teachers. It so happened that the widow's two sons were home, and the whole family assembled to be instructed by the visiting teachers. Soon the visitors began to comment on the "Thatcher episode," as it was called, and explained how unjustly Brother Thatcher had been treated. The widow answered not a word, but there was a gathering storm in her stern eyes and high-held head. After some minutes of listening to the visitors find fault with the quorum of the apostles with respect to Brother Thatcher, she slowly got up from her chair and as slowly walked to the entrance door of the house which she threw wide open. With eyes now blazing she turned to the two brethren and said: "There is the door. I want you to leave this house instantly. I will not permit anyone in this house to revile the authorities of the

Church, men laboring under divine inspiration. Nor do I wish such things spoken before my sons whom I have taught to love the leaders of the Church. And don't come back until you come in the right spirit to teach us the Gospel. Here is the door. Now go!" The visitors hurried out shamefacedly, for the widow had chastised them thoroughly. In defense of the Gospel, Sister Widtsoe knew no fear.

Widtsoe, *In the Gospel Net* (Bookcraft), pp. 81-82.

JOHN A. WIDTSOE

"Without Hesitation I Answered, Yes"

On March 17th, 1921, as I was nearing the end of my fifth year with the university,[1] my future was changed. That sunshiny morning, I had gone directly from my home, with the superintendent of buildings and grounds, to plan for a recreation area for the children of the training school of the School of Education. My office did not know of my whereabouts. When I returned about noon, I was told that Dr. Richard R. Lyman had telephoned for me repeatedly. When I called, he asked me to come to his office without delay. He took me directly to the temple into the room of the Presidency, in which, with the Twelve, they were holding their regular Thursday meeting. Even then, I did not guess the purpose of the visit. After some business items had been transacted President Grant turned to me, and told me that I had been called to fill the vacancy in the Council of the Twelve, occasioned by the death of President Anthon H. Lund. Was I willing to accept the call? There flashed before my mind the probable result: The laying aside of many a cherished desire; the constant service to the end of life; the complete change in life from that for which I had been trained. But, the biggest thing in my life was the restored gospel of Jesus Christ. It had full claim upon me. Was I worthy of the office? Could I perform its duties properly? I have always been conscious of my limitations. Question after question rushed through my mind. For a moment all time and space were mine. Then, without hesitation I answered, yes. I had never refused a call by the priesthood. It was too late to begin now. The vote of the Council was taken. Under the hands of all, President Grant ordained me at once an apostle and set me apart a member of the Council of Twelve. His accompanying blessing has always been a comfort to me. The prayer circle that followed cleared my mind. As I left the temple that day, I knew the time had come to turn my back on the projects of the past. On Sunday, the following April 3, 1921, at the General Conference of the Church, the action taken by the Presidency and Twelve was confirmed by the people, and I was sustained as a member of the Council of the Twelve.

---

[1]The University of Utah.
Widtsoe, *In a Sunlit Land*, pp. 156-57.

JOHN A. WIDTSOE

"Three Whole Days"

Since my boyhood I have known the restored gospel to be true. In my college days I had subjected it to every test known to me. Throughout my life it had made the days joyous. Doubt had fled. I possessed the Truth and understood, measurably, the pure and simple gospel of Jesus Christ.

I had studied the gospel as carefully as any science. The literature of the Church I had acquired and read. During my spare time, day by day, I had increased my gospel learning. And I had put gospel truth to work in daily life, and had never found it wanting.

The claims of Joseph Smith the Prophet had been examined and weighed. No scientific claim had received a more thorough analysis. Everywhere the divine mission of the latter-day prophet was confirmed.

The restored Church had been compared with other churches. Doctrine for doctrine, principle for principle, organization for organization, the churches had been placed side by side. Compared with the churches of the world, the Church of Jesus Christ, as restored through Joseph Smith, stood like a field of ripening grain by the side of scattering stalks. . . .

I had throughout my life from early youth an unwavering testimony of the truth of the restored gospel—the testimony of the spirit. Truth had always been my first love. In The Church of Jesus Christ of Latter-day Saints, I had found, used, and enjoyed truth.

The priesthood I had recognized as the life-giving power of the Church. Whether in quorums or in the ecclesiastical organizations it had been held in high respect by me. Those who were called to official positions, I looked upon as specially chosen for the work assigned to them. I recognized that among the offices of the priesthood the apostleship included all the divine power designed to be used for the completion of the plan of salvation and progress for men on earth. Other priesthood offices had specific limited assignments. The apostleship permitted the holder to perform any and every authorized service within the Church. Members of the Quorum of the Twelve and their associates were charged, in addition, with the responsibility of bearing witness of the truth of the glad latter-day message to all the world.

This high calling had now come to me. Faith was mine. A reasonably correct life was mine. Could I serve the cause acceptably? That was my urgent question. I knew that hundreds, perhaps thousands of men could fill the position to full satisfaction. But the call had come to me. I must seek to use my every gift for the promotion of the Lord's latter-day work. I knew that in addition I would have the Lord's help. At the best, my own powers would be inadequate. So I told the Lord, as I prayed for help, and in that spirit set out to meet the requirements that might be made of me. . . .

Two weeks after the fateful March 17, at the general conference on April 3rd, 1921, I sat on the stand and saw a sea of hands raised to sustain me, with the other General Authorities of the Church. Then I knew the die had been cast; I must enter into new activities, and travel a new road. And, I thanked the Lord for his guidance.

The first task was to provide for my family under new conditions. I had earned well for many years, and, until the university appointment, with the help of a wise wife, had been moving towards financial independence. Now, the Church allowance, supposed to be sufficient for a modest support, was about a third of what my annual earnings had been, going on two decades. My university expenses had exceeded the income. We had just built a home near the university. Our setting was made for some university years. Not much of the savings of earlier years was left. The two older children were ready for missions. There was only one thing to do: to rearrange the family mode of living to come within the reduced income. So, the automobile was sold, and the hired help was dismissed. The family did not complain. My wife, true to her pioneer ancestry and her faith in the gospel, went on under the changed conditions cheerily and with a smile.

After some years finances became somewhat easier, but have never reached the professional level of the early years. Now we can laugh at ourselves and some of the experiences of that day. For the apostleship I turned my face from the pursuit of money.

Our silver wedding anniversary came during this period. There was no money for silver, and going into debt was foreign to our code of living. Automobile there was none. So I put the whole matter up to the lady involved; and she reached a quick and possible solution. She asked that for an anniversary gift I stay with her three whole days. That was an unusual request in a household where the husband spent much time in travel and the other time in office and public service. But, in consultation with President Rudger Clawson of the Council of the Twelve, that was arranged. Then on the anniversary I asked her what we should do. She suggested that since we had no automobile we take a street-car ride. We boarded the Fort Douglas street car, and traveled to the end of the line. We had never seen the whole car line before. It was a real adventure on that glorious spring day (June 1, 1923). Other inexpensive events followed. If one so desires, great satisfaction may be found in simple pleasures. That is a lesson well to learn.

Widtsoe, *In a Sunlit Land*, pp. 158-62.

JOHN A. WIDTSOE

"I Went to the Temple to Forget the Failure"

Soon after my call to the apostleship, I was chosen a director of the Latter-day Saints Genealogical Society. . . .

My own genealogy required attention. After my mother and Aunt had filled their missions in Norway, they remained for the better part of a year to secure our genealogy. They brought home a list of about a hundred names of our dead relatives, and a book full of names of people who were probably related to us, but of their direct relationship we had no clue.

This was disappointing. Temple work was done for the names of our family. Then the matter languished.

One Sunday morning when I awoke I had a distinct impulse to examine the book the sisters had brought with them, containing the list of blood relatives that they had collected. Obedient as I have always been to spiritual messages, I sought out the book, and studied it for five hours. I found that morning the key which has enabled me to secure thousands of desired names.

The temple is peculiarly a place of revelation. Many experiences have proved it. Perhaps the most impressive is this: For several years, under a Federal grant with my staff of workers we had gathered thousands of data in the field of soil moisture; but I could not extract any general law running through them. I gave up at last. My wife and I went to the temple that day to forget the failure. In the third endowment room, out of the unseen, came the solution, which has long since gone into print.

It has been a joy to me to participate as often as possible in work for the dead. The sealing evenings when they, the long dead, have been sealed as husband and wife or children sealed to their parents have been unusually impressive.

Widtsoe, *In a Sunlit Land*, pp. 176-77.

JOHN A. WIDTSOE

"The Strange Bird Became the Object of Attention"

A flock of seagulls followed us by day and roosted in the rigging by night. On the morning of the fifth day out, a newcomer was among them. Grey-brown, long winged, larger than the gulls, with long, thin legs laid under the body and projecting beyond the tail feathers.

He flew with an effort. At times he would descend toward the water as if ready to rest upon it; then with redoubled effort he would raise himself and strive to keep up with the ship.

The strange bird became the object of attention. What kind of bird was he? Where did he come from? Why did he fly so wearily?

Spy glasses were brought out. Once, he nearly overtook the ship so he could be seen quite clearly with the naked eye. We soon concluded that it was a crane, driven from its shore-lands over the ocean by the terrific storm of the week before.

We became more interested. Cranes are wading birds, hence their long legs. To rise to flight easily their feet must touch solid ground. While the sea-gull may float upon the water and rise directly into flight, a crane would find it difficult and tend to remain afloat until it reached a shallow place where its feet could touch bottom.

What would happen to the crane? Would he weary into desperation, settle upon the water and be destroyed? Or would he save himself by attempting a landing upon the ship.

The day wore on and the bird's predicament held passengers and crew in tense suspense.

Finally, toward the end of the afternoon, the crane determined upon an effort to save himself, lengthened his body in fierce desire, beat his wings in violent regularity and strained every muscle in a sight to stir the soul. Nearer and nearer he came to the ship, reached it, hovered over it, flew almost to the first mast and then dropped heavily to the deck.

The passengers and crew rejoiced that the bird had made a wise decision and summoned sufficient energy to escape the dreary end that would have come if he had been enticed into the easier rest on the water. On the last day, when land was in sight, he was released for an easy flight to the shore to wade on solid ground.

Elder Widtsoe related this to being driven by winds of false doctrine, superstition and disobedience; humanity has settled into an ocean of error. There it drifts, finding it difficult or impossible to rise in orderly flight to a haven of happiness without solid truth beneath its feet. Once in a while, someone bends every energy to find truth and sets out to find truth after truth until he enters into the kingdom of truth and finds unspeakable joy.

Millennial Star, February 2, 1928.

Biographical Sketch

PRESIDENT BRIGHAM YOUNG, JR.

Brigham Young, Jr., was born December 18, 1836, at Kirtland, Ohio, the son of Brigham Young and Mary Ann Angell. He was ordained an apostle on February 4, 1864, by his father. He was set apart as a member of the Quorum of the Twelve on October 9, 1868, at the age of 31. Elder Young was sustained as a counselor to President Brigham Young on April 8, 1873. He was sustained as President of the Quorum of the Twelve on October 17, 1901.

Brigham Young, Jr., was born during a period of great trial in the Church. He was a twin. His twin sister, Mary, died in infancy. At age twelve he drove an ox team across the plains.

As a young man he served a mission to England and in 1864 he returned to Europe to assist President Daniel H. Wells in the presidency of the European Mission. In 1865 President Wells returned to Utah and Elder Young was appointed president of the European Mission.

Brigham Young, Jr., was a noble representative of his

father. His gentle wisdom, his merry heart, and his integrity were known to all the Saints.[1]

He died on April 11, 1903, in Salt Lake City.

[1]Susa Young Gates, "Lives of Our Leaders, the Apostles," *Juvenile Instsuctor,* May 1, 1900, pp. 260-61.

BRIGHAM YOUNG, JR.

"I'm Not Going to Lose Sight of His Wagon Wheels"

After reaching the Salt Lake Valley, President Brigham Young returned to Winter Quarters to bring the rest of his family and other pioneers to their new home in Utah. After traveling many many miles the pioneers became very tired and discouraged. Had this been any other people, there would have been mutiny and a sharp turn backward to the shelter of civilization.

Always alert to the pressure of influences about him President Young felt the resistance that manifested itself in silence rather than in words. One afternoon at three o'clock, he hitched up his coach and with the terse statement that he was "going to the valley; if anybody wants to follow, the road is open," the President put the whip to his horses and gave not a glance behind. Like a flash the boy flung the yoke upon his oxen, hitched them to his wagon, picked up his whip and drove as rapidly as he could after the coach rolling away to the west.

The determination which filled his whole soul and which stiffened the youthful lips into the iron line across his face so much like his father's was expressed in the words which he uttered to his father's wife who hastily took her seat in the wagon:

"Father's started; I'm not going to lose sight of his wagon wheels while daylight lasts." Fun may bubble, play may be fascinating, but when "father starts or leads the way," there will his son Brigham follow—even to the very courts of heaven.

Away flew the coach and one carriage and away clumsily followed the double yoke of oxen not too far behind. The storm whistled and raged, and the stiff fingers of the boy could scarcely hold the whip. But on he ran beside his oxen, urging them on with word and lash. Evening came early, and aided by the gloomy clouds overhead, the whole country was enveloped in pitchy darkness. The road would loom up in the gloom as if the little swale ahead were a precipice hundreds of feet to the bottom. Even that much light was soon absorbed in night and the storm, and the whip was lost from the half-frozen hands of the little driver as he stumbled over a stump. His body was thinly clad; he wore only a pair of jeans pants; no shoes or stockings, a thin, calico shirt, with a bit of a cape made by his mother from a coat tail, and the cape was worse than useless as it was blown constantly about his ears and head. Clinging to the bow, the boy ran beside the clumsy beasts, knowing not where he was going or what would be the end. But "father was ahead," and the boy's heart leaned upon "father" and upon the God of his father! The hours came and went in that fearful drive. . . . A light! Tis campfire! And the faithful oxen moved heavily into camp. They had traveled about eighteen miles since three o'clock and now it was just midnight!

Gates, "Lives of Our Leaders, the Apostles," *Juvenile Instructor*, May 1, 1900, pp. 260-61.

"I'll Take Father's Counsel"

In 1864, Brigham Young, Jr., was called to return to Europe to assist President Daniel H. Wells in the presidency of the European mission. Before leaving home, President Young took his son aside and said to him: "My son, you are going away upon a long and important mission. You will have heavy responsibility placed upon you, and you will not be near me so as to receive help and counsel. But there is One always near you, who will listen to your prayer and give you counsel and help. Whenever you are in doubt or trouble, go to Him in secret, and state your case fully to Him just as you would to me. He knows your desire, but there is a power in expressed or uttered prayer. You may not understand or desire the best way, and if you put your thoughts into words, the Spirit will make things plain to your mind, and teach you through your own words exactly what to pray for. Therefore, just talk to the Lord, and explain fully what you want. It is your right to receive revelation, and God will give it unto you just when and how you need it. When you seek Him you will find Him."

Many times Elder Young had occasion to recall and act upon the counsel of his father. At one time he arranged to send a large emigration to America; and for this purpose he chartered a sailing vessel for five hundred souls. If the passengers through any mischance failed to sail, he was to forfeit $100.00 a day as long as she waited. The time for sailing came perilously near; only a week remained, and as yet not one emigrant sent in his name and fee. Elder Young was in Liverpool, but as the time drew nearer still, he took the train for London to see if there were any returns received in that office. He, as well as the other brethren, were seized with dismay when they discovered that only three days remained and not a return had been made. After hours of restless anxiety, the thought flashed over the young man's mind, "I'll take father's counsel!" Upstairs he ran, and shutting himself in the upper chamber, he composed his mind, and kneeling down, told the Lord exactly the trouble which lay heavy at his heart, with the desires which accompanied his anxieties. No sooner was his prayer uttered that the answer came, "The returns will all be in, and the vessel will sail on time." He arose from his knees, assured and at perfect peace. As he came down the stairs, Bishop Thurber, who was assisting him, looked and seeing the beaming face, flew up the stairs, and catching him in his arms, said joyously, "It'll be all right," said Elder Young. And it was all right. The returns began pouring in, almost all on one mail, and every berth was taken and the vessel sailed on the appointed hour. As the company were about to sail, Elder Young blessed them, giving them many words of good and wise counsel, adding, "You will reach the other side in safety and not one soul will be buried in the ocean." Strange to say, although this prophecy was literally fulfilled, two Saints died two days after landing and were buried in New York.

Gates, "Lives of Our Leaders, the Apostles," *Juvenile Instructor*, May 1, 1900, pp. 262-63.

Index

Rigdon, Sidney, 205
Robinson, George W., 206
Roosevelt, Theodore, 245-46
Russell, Isaac, 116

Sabbath day, 6
Sacrifice, 13-16, 37, 84, 219-20, 273-74
Salvation for dead, 274-75
Samoa, 69, 71
Sarah, 13
Satan, 165
Schoenfeldt, Edward, 221
Senate, U.S., 236
Sermons, preparation of, 82
Short Creek Ranch, 103
Skanchy, Anthon L., 282, 284
Smith, Don Carlos, 229
Smith, George A., biography of, 227-28;
    stories of, 229-33
Smith, George Albert, 63, 176
Smith, Hyrum, 191
Smith, John Henry, 273
Smith, Joseph F., 18, 98, 134, 142, 255,
    272
Smith, Prophet Joseph, 112, 113, 118,
    190-91, 214-15, 227, 229, 230
Smith, Robert, 130
Smoot, Reed, biography of, 235-37;
    stories of, 239-52
Snow, Lorenzo, 33, 56, 142, 236
Sorrow, 18
Spirit world, 84-86, 117-18
Springfield, Illinois, 6
Standing, Joseph, 57

Tahiti, 70, 71, 72
Talmage, James E., biography of, 255-56;
    stories of, 257-61
Taylor, John, 33, 36, 164, 188
Taylor, Joseph E., 272
Taylor Stake, 10
Temple work, 5, 17, 165, 294
Tenney, Ammon M., 103

Tenney, Nathan C., 103, 104
Testimony, 4, 7, 11, 44, 48, 76-77, 81,
    91-93, 100-102, 120, 160-62, 205-207,
    221, 241, 242, 265, 279-82
Thatcher, Moses, 288
Theological school at Kirtland, 111
Three witnesses, 191
Thurber, Bishop, 304
Tithing, 75
Tongues, gift of, 221-22
Train, lesson from, 259-61
Truth, 291, 294-96

Unity, 73, 220, 288-90
University of Deseret, 148

Vision, 12, 208-209, 221, 266-68

Wailuku, Hawaii, 42
Walton, Mrs., 198-200
Watt, George D., 118
Welfare program, 176
Wells, Daniel H., 158, 272, 299, 303
Whitmer, David, 48-51
Whitmer, John C., 51
Whitney, Heber Kimball, 273
Whitney, Orson F., biography of, 263-64;
    stories of, 265-75
Widtsoe, Anna Gaarden, 279, 283, 284, 285,
    286
Widtsoe, John A., biography of, 277-78;
    stories of, 279-96; 239
Willes, William, 235
Word of Wisdom, 72, 250, 286
Work, 23, 124, 285
Woodruff, A. O., 250
Woodruff, Wilford, 33, 97

Young, Brigham, 30, 33, 46, 47, 79, 80,
    85, 97, 109, 114, 163, 220, 241, 251-52,
    301, 303
Young, Brigham, Jr., 272; biography of,
    299-300; stories of, 301-304
Young, John W., 55

307